101

ONE HUNDRED

AND ONE

Activities for Empathy & Awareness

101 Activities & Ideas

Sue Jennings

101 Activities for Empathy & Awareness
101 Ideas for Managing Challenging Behaviour
101 Activities for Increasing Focus & Motivation
101 Activities for Social & Emotional Resilience
101 Activities for Positive Thoughts & Feelings

HINTON HOUSE Emotional Literacy Resources

101
ONE HUNDRED · AND ONE

Activities for Empathy & Awareness

Sue Jennings

HINTON HOUSE

Dedication

To Ioana Serb, friend and practitioner

Published by

Hinton House Publishers Ltd,

Newman House, 4 High Street, Buckingham, MK18 1NT, UK

T +44 (0)1280 822557   F +44 (0)560 313 5274
E info@hintonpublishers.com

www.hintonpublishers.com

First published 2011
Reprinted 2013

Worksheet illustrations by Suzanne Hall

Printed in the United Kingdom by Hobbs the Printers Ltd

British Library Cataloguing in Publication Data

Jennings, Sue.
   101 activities for empathy & awareness. – (101 activities & ideas)
   1. Emotional problems of children. 2. Emotional problems of teenagers. 3. Emotional intelligence–
Study and teaching. 4. Social perception--Study and teaching. 5. Respect for persons–Study and
teaching. 6. Self-consciousness (Awareness)–Study and teaching.
   I. Title II. Series III. One hundred and one activities for empathy & awareness IV. Hundred and one
activities for empathy & awareness
   155.4'124-dc22

ISBN 978 1 906531 33 1

Contents

Contents

About the Author

Sue Jennings PhD is a storyteller, play and dramatherapist and trainer. She has extensive experience working with children and teenagers of all ages both in schools and the community. She travels to Malaysia, Israel, Romania and India to develop her work on Neuro-Dramatic Play, especially with groups with PDD, and those with behavioural and emotional difficulties. She has published extensively (www.suejennings.com), and her PhD thesis is also a book about the Temiar people of Malaysia.

Sue and her husband Peter are currently developing empathy and awareness projects in Romania with teenagers and young adults from the former orphanages, including groups who are living on the railway stations.

For workshops and conferences email: drsuejennings@gmail.com

Introduction

There will be many teachers, parents and others who are increasingly concerned at the apparent lack of empathy among many children and young people. Bullying appears to be on the rise, and many young people face the future with little education because of exclusions.

One of the reasons I was motivated to write this book was my own concern at the absence of positive role models, especially in sport and on television, available to set examples to the next generation. Bad behaviour is peddled for our entertainment, and soaps have shifted to greater violence and lack of basic respect. I began to do a survey of how many times the word 'grab' was present in advertising, for example: 'grab bags', 'grab and go', 'grab and fly'… and to grab something is usually a violent action.

No book is a magic formula and many other things would need to change in society in order for us to have more confident, happy and motivated young people. However, it does provide a basic structure of techniques and exercises that are graded developmentally to provide something for every young person's ability.

The philosophy of this book is grounded in attachment theory, and a belief that neglected early attachment can lead to a lack of trust and empathy (Jennings 2010). This approach suggests that early experiences can be re-worked in intensive group workshops with age-appropriate materials. It is possible for group members to move on from early deprivation and loss, and to recover a state of trust, confidence and the capacity to empathise with others.

It is essential to be able to set ground rules and eventually agree a contract with the group, whatever their age. Initially it is advisable to keep the ground rules simple and few. In my experience an initial agreement that participants do not hurt each other, either physically or verbally, and that equipment is not deliberately broken, is enough. In group discussion encourage the group to make their own suggestions for the ground rules which will eventually make up a contract between everyone, including the leader. The introduction of words such as 'respect', 'listening', 'allowing', 'differences' will gradually expand the empathic understanding of group members. However, the leader will always need some sort of device for getting the group to stop and listen, and two beats on a small drum are usually very effective.

Section 1   deals with ways of providing sensory awareness and integration through the use of play and movement. Rhythmic movement is a means of developing physical awareness and self-control, and is important in managing energy and tension. Developing the imagination begins to enable a 'problem-solving' approach.

Section 2   addresses the setting of limits and agreeing ground rules. Group members are encouraged to be aware of themselves and others, and to deal with resentments. Participants are encouraged to make personal choices and to practise leadership skills.

Section 3   begins with techniques for finding one's voice and being to communicate personal and social needs. The difference between 'reacting and responding' is clarified and issues around 'persuasion' are tackled through role-play.

Section 4   is about understanding how the past can influence the present in unhelpful ways. Group members are encouraged to build trust and deal with rejection. Stories are used to encourage empathic reactions and the offering of help to others.

Section 5   allows participants to re-visit sensory experiences and through role-play, give form to feelings. Consideration is given to family members where there are concerns. The theme of dealing with pressures is an important aspect of work with children and young people today.

The book ends with how to give feedback, making friends, preparations for leaving and saying goodbyes, and finally celebrations of achievements.

Ideally, children and young people will make the best progress if they attend a group at least twice a week, with time for 'practice' in between. However, if this is not possible, groups should be held as often as is practical, ensuring that themes covered in the previous sessions are reviewed briefly before starting. It is recommended that every session starts with the group coming together in a circle for some breathing exercises, and a few moments for any feedback from the previous session. Sessions could end by repeating coming together in the circle and voicing 'any thoughts for the journey'. Words such as 'encourage', 'suggest', 'support', 'invite' and 'reassure' are used frequently throughout this book, these themes should be kept in mind as your group progresses.

It is suggested that the sections of the book are worked through chronologically if at all possible, although you may not need, or wish, to implement every technique. Some themes will need to be repeated more than once, and it can be helpful to encourage group members to request their favourite activities.

Games can be used as a basic 'warm-up' if some of the group seem reluctant to join in. For example, throwing a light-weight football to each other as everyone says their name or how they are feeling is a very good standby to bring the group together. Traditional games such as a 'pretend three-legged race' (without ankles actually being tied together), give permission for physical touch as well as making it possible for everyone to succeed. Other games such as hopscotch, tag, catch tag, fox and lambs are just a few examples of useful ideas. Always remember to check that any games chosen are age-appropriate.

As many of these activities involve creative techniques, inevitably a large amount of art and craft work will build up over time. Each group member could have their own box or drawer where their work is kept until the end of the group. Alternatively, everyone's work could be photographed and then pictures stuck into workbooks as a record of progress. Ensure everyone has a say in what happens to their work as it should be considered personal and their intellectual property.

The Worksheets

Photocopiable worksheets are included at the end of the book to develop the work in the different sections, along with ideas for further reading.

Worksheets 1 to 11 are all linked to activities in the text, but you may also decide to adapt them to another context. For example, Worksheet 4, 'The Mask of Fear', might be used instead as 'The Mask of Anger'.

Worksheets 13 'Friendship Circles' and 14 'Friendship Tree' are not linked to specific exercises. They need to be used with care. They could, for instance, be very painful for a child who is lonely and feels they have no friends. Use these handouts once the group is well established and confident or when you wish to test the friendships within the group. You could create a whole session about friendships and include ideas from group members.

Where possible, try to facilitate this type of group with as many adult helpers as possible: volunteers, students, teaching assistants. It will enhance your work with these children and young people who have special emotional needs and often require specific developmental interventions.

Disclosures

It is possible that during an activity a group member might get distressed or make a disclosure, perhaps about abuse (during Activity 51 for example). Some individuals may be comforted within the group by their peers; others may need a follow-up session with the group leader, school counsellor or head of pastoral care. If it is a question of previously undisclosed sexual or physical abuse, then the school or centre guidelines for recording and reporting should be followed.

Part One
Before the Journey Starts

Themes

1 Sensory awareness & physical control

2 Group cooperation

3 Physical shapes & confidence

4 Physical confidence & awareness of others

5 Ease in the body & letting go of tension

6 Appropriate tension & contrasting relaxation

7 Contrasting movement & exploration of characters

8 Mastery of movement, self-control & the beginnings of character

9 Development of the sense of touch & smell

10 Re-awakening of sensory awareness in age-appropriate ways

11 Awareness of individual & others' body limits

12 Self-awareness & appropriate use of physical strengths

13 Awareness of physical limits & of the imagination

14 Awareness of self & others through physical experiences

15 Physical awareness & energy management

16 Working together & expansion of non-verbal communication

17 Group collaboration & awareness of others

18 Collaboration & cooperation

19 Awareness of others through drama games

20 Further collaborative games

1 Rhythm & Cues (i)

 Children Teenagers

> **Aims** To address issues of sensory awareness and physical control.

> **Materials** Strong drum, music for relaxation, CD player, a large white board and markers, a fleecy blanket for each person if possible.

Warm Up Bring the group together in a circle and acknowledge everyone's names. Suggest that the ground rules and contract for the group will be established later, but for now the following are the basics: i) no-one must get hurt, and ii) when the drum sounds twice, everyone must stand still and listen.

Encourage everyone to move around the room, and practice stopping when the drum sounds. Develop this into everyone running in and out of everyone else, without touching.

Focus Contrast walking with stealth and walking with noise (make scratching sounds with the drum, contrasted with loud slow beats as group move round the room); vary the speed so participants move faster and slower.

Discussion Establish the aims of the group, both for this meeting and the future (if it is a continuing group): that it will address issues of learning more about ourselves and other people; encourage confidence and communication skills, and help us look at changing the patterns of how we behave towards other people. Write the main aims on the board. Allow a brief time for questions.

Activities Return to the warm-up exercise:
- ⊗ Start in a circle, then everyone moves around the room and stops when the drum sounds.
- ⊗ Make great strides around the room, then move in very small steps.
- ⊗ Dribble an imaginary ball round the room.
- ⊗ Form pairs and pass an imaginary ball to a partner, moving down the room.
- ⊗ With a new partner, play an imaginary game of tennis.

> **Sharing** Discuss in the whole group what was fun, and encourage suggestions for more movements; emphasise how important the exercises are for coordination, rhythm and getting cues from others.

> **Ending** Invite everyone to lie down or sit on the floor, with a blanket if they wish, play relaxation music and suggest that everyone closes their eyes for five minutes.

Before the Journey Starts

Rhythm & Cues (ii)

 ✓ Children ✓ Teenagers

Aims To begin to address issues of group cooperation.

Materials Strong drum, music for relaxation, CD player, a large white board and markers, a fleecy blanket for each person if possible.

Warm Up Revisit and practise stopping and starting with the use of the drum. Introduce the idea of moving in a very rigid way and then moving in a very floppy way.

Focus Suggest people stand back-to-back and support each other while you count to ten; repeat with group members counting very quietly and becoming very loud.

Discussion Remind the group of the two basic ground rules: no-one gets hurt, and everyone must listen when the drum beats twice. Invite group members to contribute further suggestions for ground rules and write them on the board.

Introduce the idea of extremes of quality of movement, such as rigid and floppy or icy and fluid, and encourage group members to make further suggestions and write them on the board. Now introduce the idea of opposites in movement, such as different postures e.g., small and tall.

Activities Working with the whole group, as you make small drum beats invite everyone to:
- ✪ Stand as wide and tall as they can and take up as much room as possible.
- ✪ Stand as small as they can and take up as little room as possible.
- ✪ Move slowly from the small position to the tall position and back again, and repeat several times.
- ✪ Introduce a feeling into the postures: very small and scared, very large and scary.
- ✪ Develop further: very small and scary, very large and scared.

Sharing With the whole group, discuss what was easy, what was difficult, what was fun, write the responses on the board; invite suggestions for the next group session.

Ending Invite everyone to lie down or sit on the floor, with a blanket if they wish, play relaxation music and suggest that everyone closes their eyes for five minutes.

Before the Journey Starts

3 Stretch & Shake (i)

☑ Children   ☑ Teenagers

> **Aims** To encourage physical qualities and shapes, and confidence.

> **Materials** Strong drum, music for relaxation, CD player, a large white board and markers, a fleecy blanket for each person if possible.

Warm Up Ask whether the group remember the ground rules and allow a short time for individuals to contribute. Add any new ideas they think would be useful.

Ask everyone to stand in a circle and give a big stretch upwards, hands and fingers reaching towards the ceiling, then repeat towards each sides (ensure space is negotiated with others); repeat three or four times.

Now everyone can shake out their hands, then their arms, one foot then the other; moves their head slowly from side to side. Now try to shake the whole body at once.

Focus Beat the drum slowly as the group walk slowly round the room; invite people to repeat the walk in time with a partner.

Discussion Check if there is anything arising from the previous session that people want to discuss, and repeat anything new for the ground rules, which can be written on the board.

Activities In the previous session the group moved with different postures of movement, now explore different shapes of movement such as:

- ✪ Everyone moving around the room with spiky moves, not just using the fingers but the whole body, then change to straight movement.
- ✪ Explore the difference between round and square movements.
- ✪ Working with a partner, elaborate the movements together, one person mirroring the other and then swap over.
- ✪ Working together with a partner, create a sequence of spiky, straight, round and square movements.

> **Sharing** In the whole group, discuss how people felt making the different movements; and invite suggestions and any new ideas for development.

> **Ending** Invite everyone to lie down or sit on the floor, with a blanket if they wish, play relaxation music and suggest that everyone closes their eyes for five minutes. Introduce the idea of a gentle breathing exercise as people relax: 'Breath in slowly through your nose and breath out slowly through your mouth.'

Stretch & Shake (ii)

✓ Children ⭕ Teenagers

Aims To build up physical confidence and gradual awareness of others.

Materials Strong drum, music for relaxation, CD player, a large white board and markers, a fleecy blanket for each person if possible.

Warm Up Run around the room to fast drum beats, then gradually slow to a walk; skip to the drum beat (some youngsters may need coaching for this) and then skip with a partner; partners can help each other to learn skipping; pause, and then everyone stretches up high, gives a big yawn, stretches wide and gives another yawn, and then shakes all over like a jelly!

Focus Stay in pairs and help each other to balance on one leg, and then finish with a good shake together.

Discussion Begin with a reminder of the contract, and start to evolve aims with the group: write the first one: 'To feel better about myself' on the board, and add others if suggested.

Activities Ask everyone to sit in a circle and clap as an echo to the drum beat:

- ⊗ Start with a slow '1, 2, 1, 2' beat and ask the group to clap in response.

- ⊗ Extend this to '1, 2, 3 pause, 1, 2, 3 pause'.

- ⊗ Now form pairs, standing one behind the other, one person is the drum and the other echoes the drum rhythm, by beating it on 'the drum's' back. Emphasise that only the area between the shoulders and waist should be used and that it is possible to 'beat' a rhythm using gentle patting or tapping.

- ⊗ Encourage group members to compose a simple rhythm by clapping or working with their partner tapping on backs.

- ⊗ Allow each pair to play a 'back rhythm', changing over so each person has a turn.

Sharing Encourage feedback from everyone, thinking about what they did or didn't like.

Ending Suggest that everyone curls up in a blanket and feels warm and safe, while they close their eyes; be aware of breathing, in through the nose and out through the mouth.

Before the Journey Starts

5 Tension Release (i)

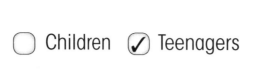

○ Children ✓ Teenagers

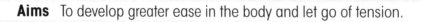

Aims To develop greater ease in the body and let go of tension.

Materials Strong drum, CD player, a large board and markers.

Warm Up Make use of the drum to create a sense of escalation as you invite everyone to breath in, more, more, more – and then imagine a feeling of bursting into pieces; repeat several times. Do a 'footballer's warm up' by skipping round the room, then several stretches, both legs – pressing forward on the knee and back on the heel; both arms – reaching up and behind to stretch the elbow. Ask for suggestions from the group for stretching techniques.

Focus Suggest that everyone lies on the floor and stretches out as far as possible to take up maximum space and then slowly curls up as small as possible – repeat twice.

Discussion Start to finalise the ground rules that people think are appropriate for the group, and encourage contributions of personal aims for their time in the group. Are there particular things that people would like to achieve through attending the sessions?

Activities Invite people to work in pairs and develop a sequence of mirror movements:

⊗ One person makes a move and the other copies it, then change over.

⊗ Now each person adds a second movement. Put the two movements together, one mirroring the other.

⊗ Now each add a third movement – develop these gradually so that the mirroring has time to be accurate.

⊗ Now try doing each person's full sequence at exactly the same time, first one step, then two, then three.

Sharing Put the three movements from each person (i.e., six movements) together in a sequence and show it to the rest of the group.

Ending Discuss in the whole group what it felt like to share their work. If the group enjoy the relaxation sequence, then provide music, and blankets if available.

Before the Journey Starts

Tension Release (ii)

6

 ☑ Children   ☑ Teenagers

> **Aims**   To develop an awareness of appropriate tension and contrasting relaxation.

> **Materials**   Strong drum, music for relaxation, CD player, a large white board and markers, a fleecy blanket for each person if possible.

Warm Up   Walk across the room as if it is a muddy swamp, then very slippery ice, then a stony beach with bare feet; contrast with walking in the soft sand, a deep soft carpet, a springy grass field.

Focus   Teenagers: play an imaginary game of ice hockey with a partner, then relax in front of a warm fire. Children: play an imaginary game of snowballs, then relax in front of a warm fire.

Discussion   Encourage everyone to think about and discuss times when can tension be important: e.g., in certain sports, when we are alert to danger, and so on. Write the answers on the board.

Activities   In the whole group, encourage everyone to mime the following:

⊗ A tug of war: split into two groups and pull an imaginary rope in opposite directions.

⊗ Develop this with first one side 'winning' then the other and showing their triumph.

⊗ Develop this still further by pretending there is a lot of tension (set face and teeth, tense muscles, brace legs and so on).

⊗ Extend the show with the winners being thrilled and the losers dejected – all in mime and using as little tension as possible.

> **Sharing**   Discuss in the whole group whether it is really possible to be convincing when pretending to perform physical activities. What might be missing?

> **Ending**   Invite everyone to sit or lie down, with a blanket if they wish, and first tense every muscle as hard as they can, and then relax 'like melted butter' and close their eyes.

Before the Journey Starts

7 Loopy Loo & Stretchy Steve

✓ Children ○ Teenagers

Aims To encourage children to develop their movement in contrasting ways, and to explore characters.

Materials Music for relaxation, CD player, a large white board and markers, a fleecy blanket for each person if possible.

Warm Up Loopy Loo is very bendy and can only just stand up to walk: move round the room as Loopy, very floppy, like a rag doll. Stretchy Steve is tall and straight and reaches out, sometimes to the sky, sometimes to the sides and sometimes in front: stretch like Steve in all directions.

Focus Move from being very stretchy to very floppy and back again, from Loopy Loo to Stretchy Steve.

Discussion In the whole group, explore different words that describe how we move, such as lazily, briskly, heavily, stiffly; write the words on the board

Activities Working with the whole group, develop the words written on the board through movement:

 ✪ Loopy is trying to move briskly with great difficulty, then Steve is trying to be more bendy.

 ✪ Working in twos, Loopy and Steve move together in a lazy way, then in a heavy way.

 ✪ Encourage the pairs to have a 'movement conversation' as one moves and then the other, in different ways.

Sharing Encourage everyone to contribute to a group discussion about what they found fun in the session, and suggest ideas for the future.

Ending Invite everyone to lie down and give a big stretch like Steve, right through their whole bodies, and then to go floppy like Loopy; curl up under the blanket and listen to the music.

Animal Magic

☑ Children ☑ Teenagers

Aims To develop mastery of movement, self-control and the beginnings of character.

Materials Pictures of different animals to stimulate ideas for movement such as: dolphin, elephant, tiger, snake, eagle, mouse, wolf; strong drum, music for relaxation, CD player, large white board and markers.

Warm Up Suggest that everyone closes their eyes and chooses an animal, it can be small or large, wild or tame, it can be on the earth, in the sea or in the air; encourage everyone to move like their animal, first slowly and then fast, slow and then fast; move as if their animal is angry, then sleepy, and then stop.

Focus Everyone must decide on one typical movement of their animal and then 'freeze' like a picture.

Discussion In the whole group, explore different words that describe how we move, such as stiffly, smoothly, heavily, lightly; write all the words on the board. Invite everyone to look at the animal pictures and suggest words to describe how they move, and write these on the board. Find out if people have seen wildlife programmes and what they noticed about animal movements.

Activities Working with the whole group, suggest various types of movement for everyone to explore:

- ⊗ Move like a dolphin playing in the water, a tiger stalking its prey, an elephant drinking water (vary the language for children and teenagers).
- ⊗ Work with a partner and choose two animals that move together and then chase each other.
- ⊗ With a partner create a still picture of an animal for the rest of the group to guess and then copy the same posture.

Sharing Invite the group to suggest possible stories that could develop from the animal movements.

Ending Invite everyone to sit back-to-back with their partner, close their eyes and relax, while listening to the music.

Before the Journey Starts

9 Lotions & Potions (i)

☑ Children   ◯ Teenagers

> **Aims**   To encourage the development of the senses of touch and smell.

> **Materials**   Baby lotion; a basket of cotton wool pieces dabbed with essential oils; a small basket with sprigs of fresh herbs, e.g., sage, thyme, lemon-grass; a fleecy blanket for everyone; a drum; large board and markers.

Warm Up   Encourage everyone to play stop-start: move around the room and stop when you play two drum beats; sit with a partner and hold hands and rock backwards and forwards, first slowly then faster and slower again; suggest that people measure their hands against their partner's and see if they are the same size.

Focus   Invite everyone to have a dab of baby lotion, rub it into their hands and smell it.

Discussion   Discuss how everyone feels tense sometimes and how shoulders can feel tense too. Tell the group that they are going to discover ways to feel more relaxed through massage. Introduce a new ground rule that the only body areas to be used for massage are on the back from shoulders to waist, and the hands. Introduce a discussion about the smells the group like and write suggestions on the board.

Activities   Invite everyone to get up and have a stretch (Stretchy Steve) and a shake-out and then sit in a circle:

- ✪ Pass round the basket of scented cotton wool and suggest everyone has a small sniff and tries to guess what the smells are. Compare the smells and discuss which people like and don't like.

- ✪ Give everyone some more baby lotion and show them how to massage their hands. Both hands together, rubbing in circles, individual fingers (not using a pulling motion but round and round), then the backs, always stroking towards the body and not away.

- ✪ Pass round the basket of herbs for everyone to smell and guess what they are and whether they like them or not.

> **Sharing**   Suggest that everyone holds hands in the circle and rubs the hands they are holding so they get an extra massage.

> **Ending**   Give each person a piece of cotton wool with lavender oil, and suggest they can smell it while they sit back-to-back with their partner and relax, listening to the music.

Before the Journey Starts

Lotions & Potions (ii)

◯ Children ☑ Teenagers

> **Aims** To re-awaken sensory awareness in age-appropriate ways.

> **Materials** Non-perfumed hand lotion that is neutral for gender, cotton wool dabbed with essential oils, a box of textures for guessing: pieces of sandpaper, velvet, jute/hessian, fur fabric and so on; relaxation music; board and markers; Worksheet 1.

Warm Up Encourage everyone to try a 'body-percussion' where they make lots of noise: beating chests, Tarzan sounds, popping cheeks, clapping cheeks, clapping hands and elbows, bent arms and knees, bird whistles, wolf howls, owl hoots.

Focus Invite everyone to discuss and set the scene for a spooky play: everything is very quiet, then a wolf howls in the distance, nearby an owl is hooting.

Discussion Name the five senses: touch, smell, sight, taste and hearing, and talk about the evolutionary aspects of our sensory system and how it was essential for survival, e.g., if humans could not hear the crack of a twig they might become an animal's meal. Write the five senses on the board, along with any ideas from the group about their importance for survival.

Activities Some of these exercises may need to be experimented with, be aware that for some teenagers they could be embarrassing or mean loss of face. Allow people to do as much as they feel comfortable with.

- ✪ Sit with a partner and discuss the most unpleasant smell experience you can remember, and massage your own hands (with or without cream) as you are talking.
- ✪ Learn to recognise different parts of your hand and how to 'read palms'. (See Worksheet 1).
- ✪ Give each pair a piece of cotton wool and see if they can identify the smell of the essential oil.
- ✪ In the whole group, pass round the sensory box and encourage people to close their eyes or look away, then take something out and name it through touch.

> **Sharing** Invite the whole group to discuss what things they have enjoyed or disliked; and any strong memories of senses from the past.

> **Ending** Invite everyone to sit back-to-back and listen to the relaxation music, with closed eyes if possible.

Before the Journey Starts

11 Reaching & Rolling (i)

 Children ✓ Teenagers

Aims To help group members to be aware of their body limits and those of others.

Materials Large drum, relaxation music, CD player.

Warm Up Vary the run-around and shake-out with suggestions to run and jump over an imaginary river, push your way through a very thick wood, walk across a frozen lake.

Focus Working in threes, two people hold hands and the third has to find a way into the middle, without anyone getting hurt or tickled!

Discussion Explain that the group activities are becoming more difficult and that people are going to learn the skills to use their strength appropriately; the drum will be used to stop any activity that seems to be getting out of control; invite comments or questions.

Activities Suggest that everyone lies on their backs on the floor, with space around them, and stretches out with a loud yawn:

- ✪ Slowly roll over onto fronts and again stretch and yawn, curl up as small as possible, and uncurl and stretch. Repeat until a pattern is established.

- ✪ Roll over and over three times without touching anyone else, roll back three times.

- ✪ Working with a partner, one person (gently) pushes and the other person rolls, three times; repeat rolling the other way by pulling the person. Change over.

- ✪ Repeat the exercise with one person lying very rigid as if they are stuck to the floor, their partner must try to roll them against the pressure. Change over.

- ✪ Repeat with one person completely floppy so it takes an effort to roll them over. Change over.

Sharing Encourage everyone in the group to contribute their experiences of being 'pushed around' by someone else.

Ending Suggest that everyone sits back-to-back with their partner, closes their eyes and listens to the relaxation music.

Before the Journey Starts

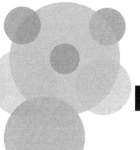

Reaching & Rolling (ii)   12

✓ Children ✓ Teenagers

> **Aims** To increase self-awareness and appropriate use of physical strengths.

> **Materials** Large drum, relaxation music, fleecy blankets.

Warm Up Suggest that half the group form a forest and the other half push their way through the branches, then change over; half the group lie on their fronts to form a swamp and the others walk across the room using the spaces in between, change over.

Focus Invite the whole group to lie down side by side, and when they hear a drum beat to roll over at the same time; repeat slowly until the group can synchronize together. With younger or less able groups begin by telling them which way to roll if necessary.

Discussion Encourage a discussion of personal strengths and events that might trigger 'explosions' and lead things to get out of control in a physical way.

Activities The rolling exercises can be developed in more complex ways:

- ✪ Everyone lies down at one end of the room and rolls over to the other end without touching anybody else.

- ✪ Each person lies flat on their front and pulls themselves along the floor to the other end of the room.

- ✪ Imagine that the floor is a difficult rock-face and that the group are climbing it slowly using their hands, knees and feet (while lying flat on the floor).

- ✪ Form pairs, and half the group 'climb the rock' while their partner pulls an imaginary rope to help them up.

> **Sharing** Encourage a discussion comparing what it is like to 'do things for real' and 'doing things in the imagination or pretending'.

> **Ending** Suggest that everyone lies down, closes their eyes and listens to the relaxation music, with a blanket if they wish.

Before the Journey Starts

13 Push Me – Pull You (i)

 ✓ Children ✓ Teenagers

> **Aims** To continue the development of awareness of physical limits and of the imagination.

> **Materials** Large drum, relaxation music.

Warm Up Encourage people to walk around the room as if they are carrying a huge weight on their shoulders, then let the weight drop and walk freely; then walk as if they are balancing something heavy on their heads and then gently lift it down and walk on.

Focus Imagine that someone is standing on your shoulders and you are walking across a tight-rope, being very careful with your balance.

Discussion Encourage the group to discuss the extremes of physical activity and what it does to our bodies: extreme sports, marathons, endurance tests; contrast extreme activities that people choose to do, and those people are obliged to do, e.g., women in India carrying bricks on their heads and damaging their spines.

Activities Ask everyone to find a partner who is approximately the same height. Warn that these activities are about being strong but controlled.

- ✪ Stand back-to-back and shake shoulders to massage each other's backs.
- ✪ Face each other and place both hands on your partner's shoulders, now both push to see if who can push their partner across the room.
- ✪ Now encourage everyone to take a firm stance, spreading their toes and keeping the strength in their legs, and try pushing shoulders again.
- ✪ With partners, create a mock struggle where pairs push each other to look as if they are fighting.
- ✪ Use the drum beat, if necessary, to assist pairs to count to three as they take it in turns to push.

> **Sharing** Each pair can show their struggle to the rest of the group; followed by a group discussion about to make things look real when they are really pretend.

> **Ending** Suggest everyone sits back-to-back with their partner, breathes deeply several times, in through the nose and out through the mouth, and listens to the relaxation music.

Before the Journey Starts

Push Me – Pull You (ii)   14

✓ Children   ✓ Teenagers

Aims To develop further awareness of self and others through physical experiences.

Materials Large drum, rhythmic music, Worksheet 2

Warm Up Imagine crossing a swamp and finding only a few firm patches of firm ground to step on; run around the room and come to a bridge that has broken, with a gap just wide enough to jump over; working with a partner, imagine one person is crossing on stepping stones and the other is holding their hand to help them balance but also to pull them across, then change over. Drum beats can be used to pace the exercises and also to stop-start if necessary.

Focus Stand facing a partner and clasp hands, lean back and see how far arms can stretch out while still keeping balanced. Emphasise that partners must look after each other and no-one is to be dropped onto a hard surface.

Discussion Encourage a discussion about balance and what it takes to get the right balance in life. Which are the most difficult things to manage to balance? (See Worksheet 2).

Activities Suggest that everyone works with a partner of the same height. Warn that these activities are about being strong but controlled.

- ✪ Lean back-to-back, and trust partners to support each other.
- ✪ Face your partner and hold hands, now try to pull your partner across the room.
- ✪ Now repeat the exercise while standing with your feet firmly on the ground, spreading the toes and using the strength in your legs, and trying pulling each other across the room again.
- ✪ Try the exercise again using only one hand.
- ✪ Create a mock struggle with each partner pulling alternately, accompanied by drumbeats if needed. Repeat until it looks spontaneous.

Sharing Encourage each pair to show their struggle to the group and then have a general discussion about how to make the struggles look more real; perhaps thinking about facial expressions?

Ending Sit back-to-back and practice deep breathing in a regular rhythm.

Before the Journey Starts

15 Bursting the Balloon (i)

○ Children ✓ Teenagers

> **Aims** To further develop physical awareness and management of energy.

> **Materials** Large drum, large balloons, large play parachute.

Warm Up Practice steady breathing with everyone blowing up a balloon and tying the top, blow up enough for one each, with two or three left over.

Focus Ask everyone to curl up on the floor until they are pricked with an imaginary pin, and then 'burst' with as much noise as possible.

Discussion Encourage the sharing of ideas for stories about balloons and other objects than can float away or be grounded.

Activities Ask everyone to hold the handles of the parachute:

- ✪ Waft the parachute upwards so that it fills with air and let it fall again, repeat several times.

- ✪ Waft the parachute up as high as possible and then all let go at the same time, at a signal, and allow it to drop.

- ✪ Everyone sits on a balloon, see who can sit and balance the longest without the balloon bursting.

- ✪ Sit on the balloons again, and this time try to break them, using only your weight.

> **Sharing** Encourage group members to suggest different ways for the balloons and the parachute to be used, and, if time, try some of them out or agree to try them in the next session (try to include everyone's ideas).

> **Ending** Invite the whole group to sit back-to-back and close their eyes and breathe deeply.

Before the Journey Starts

Bursting the Balloon (ii) 16

☑ Children   ◯ Teenagers

> **Aims**   To engage children in working together in a fun way and to expand their non-verbal communication.

> **Materials**   Large drum, strong balloons, coloured markers, fleecy blankets.

Warm Up   Ask everyone to curl up small and then imagine they are a balloon being blown up with a pump, so they expand and get bigger and bigger, soon everyone is standing up and floating round the room; on the count of three, a pin will burst them all and everyone will explode and end up on the floor again. Blow up the balloons, enough for two each and a few left over.

Focus   Encourage everyone to form small groups of three or four; give each group one balloon that they must try to keep in the air.

Discussion   Talk in the whole group about how we can sometimes get so angry that we feel as if we are going to burst and how we can explode with anger sometimes; ask everyone to contribute their own feelings of bursting with anger or frustration.

Activities   Invite the group to form pairs and to imagine that one person is the balloon and the other will blow them up: an expansion of the warm-up exercise.

- ☻ One person in each pair is the balloon and curls up small on the floor while their partner 'blows them up', as they get bigger and bigger, almost floating away, the tops are tied, and their partner takes an imaginary pin and counts to three, and bursts the balloon, shouting 'BANG!'. Change over and then repeat several times.

- ☻ Create a large balloon with half the group forming a circle and the other half blowing them up and bursting them; change over. Repeat several times.

- ☻ Give each person a balloon and some coloured markers to draw a face on it; use the balloon like a puppet to have a conversation with partners.

> **Sharing**   Encourage everyone to talk with their partners about whether the balloon-puppets are feeling that they might burst with anger, why this might be, and whether they need someone they can talk with. Finally, allow everyone to burst their balloon.

> **Ending**   Invite everyone to wrap themselves in a blanket and sit back-to-back with their partner while they relax and breathe deeply.

17   If the Cap Fits...

 Children   Teenagers

Aims   To encourage group collaboration and awareness of others.

Materials   Strong beach ball, enough different hats or caps for the whole group.

Warm Up   Encourage everyone to throw the beach ball to each other using both hands; then try to keep the ball in the air. Once this has been mastered, move around the room still trying to keep the ball in the air.

Focus   Invite everyone to choose a hat and think about who might wear it.

Discussion   Encourage everyone to talk about how teams work and play together and the meaning of the phrase 'to keep your eye on the ball'.

Activities   Invite the group to stand in a circle and look carefully around at everyone else; explain that on the count of three everyone must look at one person on the other side of the group, if that person is looking back, change places.

- ✪ Repeat this game several times so that everyone has a chance to change places.

- ✪ Make the game more difficult with everyone wearing a hat, and then changing hats when they change places.

- ✪ Take turns to stand in the circle wearing a hat or cap and perform an action that someone wearing it might do, for example a person wearing the chef's hat might start mixing food.

- ✪ Find a person wearing a hat or cap that might work with you and create an action together.

Sharing   Encourage the group to talk about how a costume can help us to play a role, and discuss the different characters people thought of while wearing their hats.

Ending   Suggest that everyone sits down with their eyes closed, and thinks about the hat they wore, and whether there are others they would like to try.

Before the Journey Starts

Together We Survive... 18

✓ Children ✓ Teenagers

Aims To increase skills of collaboration and cooperation.

Materials Large drum.

Warm Up Encourage the group to form pairs and then pretend to be in a three-legged race, first walking and then running (without tying ankles).

Focus Encourage people to practice performing an action together as a group, for example singing the same song. For younger groups, it can be easier start on a small group basis before working together as the whole group.

Discussion Invite everyone to contribute to a discussion about the importance of doing something at the same time – when it is important in a precise way (rowing in a team, singing in a choir) and in a general way (playing a team game, working on a factory line).

Activities Ask the group to form pairs and work together with their partner to:

⊗ Create a sequence of three actions that they can do at precisely the same time, such as march on the spot 4 times, jump twice and wave their right hands.

⊗ Complete the sentence 'Holidays should be ...' and then say it at exactly the same time.

⊗ Put together a 'routine' of actions, sounds or songs that can be repeated; then show the sequence to the group.

Sharing Have a whole group discussion about whether people found the joint activities enjoyable. Ensure that you feed back to the group that everyone improved with practice, as some people may find working together difficult.

Ending Suggest that everyone sits back-to-back with their partner, breathes deeply and thinks about the activities.

19 Bounces & Beats (i)

☑ Children ☑ Teenagers

> **Aims** To further develop awareness of others through simple drama games.

> **Materials** Large drum, two strong beach balls, white board and coloured markers.

Warm Up Encourage everyone to throw the beach ball to each other with arms above their heads; then look at one person and throw the ball to someone else; introduce a second ball and continue with both being thrown at once.

Focus Ask everyone to be aware of their heart beat and pulse, and think about whether these are increasing with more activity.

Discussion Encourage everyone to contribute ideas about what we notice about other people: Is it what they wear? What they do? How they look? When might we act on something we notice about another person, such as offering to carry someone's shopping, opening the door for someone carrying lots of bags or helping a child who had fallen over.

Activities Invite everyone to form a large circle with space between each person; then look round and acknowledge everyone in the group. Explain that these activities must be done one person at a time, and if two people act together, then the game must start again from the beginning. Everyone must think about and watch how others are acting.

- ✪ One by one, everyone must take one step into the circle until they form a smaller circle. This will take several attempts as people always start to move at the same time.

- ✪ Everyone must sit down one at a time until the whole group is seated.

- ✪ Write the words of a well-known song on the board and practice going round the circle with everyone saying one word. Repeat until the song flows!

> **Sharing** Suggest that everyone sits with a partner and tries to have a conversation with each person alternately saying one word.

> **Ending** Encourage everyone to sit back-to-back with their partner, breathe deeply and be aware of the other person's breathing.

Before the Journey Starts

Bounces & Beats (ii)

✓ Children   ✓ Teenagers

Aims   To re-affirm the basics of collaboration before moving on to more complex themes.

Materials   Large drum, large parachute, beach ball, tennis-sized ball, board and markers.

Warm Up   Encourage everyone to work with a partner and chase round the room, creating 'statues' when the drum is beaten twice.

Focus   Stand in the circle with the large parachute and waft it high up and down again several times, as a rhythm develops, think about how this needs everyone to be working together to make it happen.

Discussion   Invite everyone to think about the various activities from the previous sessions and write them on the board; remind people of any that have been forgotten; discuss those that have been enjoyed and whether they have made a difference to how people feel.

Activities   Ask everyone to form a circle round the parachute, and waft it as high as possible without letting go, and then bring it to the ground again:

- ✪ Place the beach ball on the parachute and practice rolling it from one side to the other; then practice matching colours: rolling red to red, yellow to yellow and so on.

- ✪ Use the parachute to try and bounce the beach ball as high as possible.

- ✪ Using the smaller ball, roll it from side to side and then to matching colours, and then between different colours such as from yellow to red.

- ✪ Waft the parachute from high and low again and then let it go when it is very high.

Sharing   Ask each person to tell the group one thing that has been important to them in the activities so far.

Ending   Form groups of four and sit all leaning against each other to relax and be still.

Before the Journey Starts

Part Two
Understanding Myself

Themes

21 Getting to Know the Group

 Children ✓ Teenagers

Understanding Myself

> **Aims**   To help a new group to establish communication.

> **Materials**   Football or beach ball, smaller balls - one for each member of the group.

Warm Up   Stand in a circle, bounce the football into the centre and say your name, someone else catches the ball, calls their name, bounces the ball and so on; repeat until everyone knows each other's names; if the group already knows each other, they can call another person's name who must catch the ball when it is bounced.

Focus   Standing in a circle, tell the group that each person must take one step forward, but this must be one person at a time, if two people step together, then the game must start again (this encourages people to be aware of each other's movements).

Discussion   In the whole group, discuss how the main aim of this group is to enable everyone to feel a part of it, to be included in all activities and to be heard when they wish to say something.

Activities   With a partner, throw and catch one small ball, then add another so two balls are thrown and caught at the same time; at the signal find a new partner and repeat.

- ✪ In the whole group, using the football or beach ball, try to keep it in the air for as long as possible, using hands only.
- ✪ For children: 'Fox and Lambs': one person is Fox and chases the Lambs, who can only stay safe by hugging one other person, but only for a count of three, if you are caught you become Fox. For teenagers vary this to 'Wolf and Lambs', the lambs stay safe by standing back-to-back for a count of three.

> **Sharing**   Talk as a group about what people did or did not enjoy about the activities, was the ball throwing game easier with some people than others? How did it feel to work together to stay safe from Fox?

> **Ending**   Everyone looks round the group, and then calls out their own name very loudly and then very quietly.

Agreeing the Contract (i)

☑ Children ☑ Teenagers

Aims To establish the 'why' and the 'how' of the group.

Materials White board with coloured markers.

Warm Up Using only the words 'empathy' and 'sympathy', create a rhythm together, chant the words and move round the room, walking and rapping.

Focus With a partner create a rhythm using the two words that you can perform together.

Discussion What are the differences in meaning between the words 'empathy' and 'sympathy'? Write the words and meanings on the white board.

Activities Practice listening skills in the group as each person takes it in turns to say what they would like to happen during the group sessions, and how they feel the group could develop; making suggestions for themes and skills, for example.

⊗ Write everyone's responses on the board, however simple they may be.

⊗ Practice 'empathic listening skills' as a story is read out (for examples of suitable stories see Resources). Suggest the everyone thinks about one character in the story and how they might be feeling.

Sharing Which character in the story did people feel empathy towards? What other words describe how people felt towards any other characters.

Ending Share with a partner what you have experienced in the group today and discuss the ground rules you think the group needs to agree.

Understanding Myself

23 Agreeing the Contract (ii)

 Children ☑ Teenagers

Aims To establish the ground rules for the group.

Materials White board with markers, paper and pens.

Warm Up Create a chant of 'Yes, you can!' and 'No, you can't!' and move round the room in rhythm.

Focus In pairs, first place hands on each other's shoulders and try to push partners across the room; then hold hands and try to pull the partners across the room. Encourage everyone to work within acceptable limits and not just to use the exercise as a show of strength.

Discussion Why do we have rules? For whose benefit? What sort of rules do the group not like?

Activities Discuss any ideas for ground rules that people have thought about since the previous session.

- ✪ Choose a topic, such as 'What I watched on TV last night' – then tell everyone to speak at once. Repeat the exercise with people speaking one at a time.

- ✪ Discuss the ground rules for the group and write them on the board (see Introduction for suggestions); include suggestions from the group where appropriate, explain/discuss those that are not appropriate.

Sharing Discuss everyone's feelings about having very clear rules, how did it feel when everyone was talking at once?

Ending Ask everyone to write down on their own sheet of paper the rules they think they will find most difficult to keep.

My Body is Me!

 Children ☑ Teenagers

> **Aims** To affirm identity and a sense of self through the body.

> **Materials** Age-appropriate music, CD player; chiffon or silk scarves in bright colours.

Warm Up Ask the whole group to shake out and relax the whole body; now form pairs to perform slow-motion 'shadow' movements – one person makes a movement then their partner copies it in slow motion to make the movement larger.

Focus Discuss with partners – what is the best thing about my body: Is it to do with strength? Looks? Flexibility?

Discussion In the whole group, think about ways of keeping our bodies relaxed so we don't get tense when we are anxious.

Activities In small groups, create a 'folk-style' dance using the scarves and music. Some teenagers, especially boys, might be reluctant to do this, if so, the word dance need not be used (nor the scarves); but emphasise the rhythm, and encourage stamping and even a shouting accompaniment. Point out that there are many vigorous Greek dances that women are not allowed to perform!

⊗ Ask everyone to imagine that they have to perform for other people and to put a little extra into their dance.

⊗ Work in pairs, one kneeling and clapping, while the other whirls around getting faster and faster, then change over.

> **Sharing** In small groups, talk about how it felt to perform the folk dance, and how working as a whole and not just as individuals can make us feel good about ourselves and about the way our bodies move.

> **Ending** Relax sitting back-to-back with a partner while gently handling the scarves and feeling the texture of the material.

Understanding Myself

25 My Body in Space (i)

☑ Children ◯ Teenagers

Understanding Myself

> **Aims** To understand how much space we need around us in order to feel safe.

> **Materials** Large pieces of material (about half the size of a single sheet) in different colours including see-through; age-appropriate music and CD player.

Warm Up Encourage everyone to skip or run round the room and then freeze at your signal; now ask them to freeze at a distance from everyone else that feels comfortable; repeat but this time at a distance that is not comfortable; repeat again at a comfortable distance.

Focus Sit with a partner at a distance that feel OK and not too crowded or too distant.

Discussion Explore how sometimes we feel that people are 'in our faces' and the times when we would prefer to have more space around us.

Activities Stand with a partner 'at arm's length' and see how this feels – too close or too distant?

⊗ In pairs, take each side of a piece of material and move round the room, keeping it taught and flat all the time.

⊗ Roll up the material diagonally so it is longer to give more space, then fold it into four to give less space. Find different ways of moving round the room, while still holding the material.

⊗ One person walks with the see-through material over their heads and their partner follows them, does this change the feeling of space around you? Change over.

> **Sharing** Which of these ways of moving felt most comfortable, with more or less distance between you? Do you and your partner feel the same?

> **Ending** Curl up on one of the pieces of material and be aware of the edges and how much space you have.

My Body in Space (ii)

26

 ☑ Children ☑ Teenagers

> **Aims** To understand how close we need to feel to others.

> **Materials** Play parachute, a fleecy blanket for each person.

Warm Up Ask everyone to hold the handles of the parachute and raise it up as high as possible and then bring it down again – practice until everyone synchronises together.

Focus Ask everyone to close their eyes and imagine different situations where other people are too close or not close enough, such as sitting in assembly, or being in a crowd at a concert or football match, or when being hugged by someone in your family.

Discussion If we feel we need more closeness, when is it appropriate to hug someone else? For children talk about friends and family, for teenagers explore 'mixed messages' when hugging others.

Activities Using the parachute, establish an up and down rhythm, and then play a game where at a signal people have to change places under the parachute before it comes down again.

⊗ Use colours, names beginning with certain letters, footwear and so on as the basis for changing place.

⊗ When the parachute is raised for the last time everyone has to try to sit in the middle before it comes down again.

⊗ As different categories are called out, everyone comes out from under the parachute, for example everyone in blue, everyone with glasses, and so on.

> **Sharing** Discuss in the whole group how the parachute games felt, were other people too close or was it just right? Sometimes moving under the parachute with others can feel crowded, and several people can end up in the same place.

> **Ending** Give everyone a blanket, so they can wrap it round themselves and relax for a few minutes.

Understanding Myself

ⓅThis page may be photocopied for instructional use only. *101 Activities for Empathy & Awareness* © Sue Jennings 2011

29

27   This is MY Name!

☑ Children   ◯ Teenagers

> **Aims**   To strengthen a feeling of identity.

> **Materials**   Thick crayons or coloured pens, A5 or A4-sized sheets of paper.

Warm Up   In the whole group play some energising name games, e.g., 'If your name begins with "M" sit down; if your name begins with "S" make a bridge' and so on. Call out different letters and physical tasks while everyone keeps walking round the room.

Focus   Working with a partner, call out your names, one after the other and make a chant and stamp your feet to the rhythm.

Discussion   Do you really like your name? Were you named after someone else? In groups discuss what people know about their names.

Activities   Ask everyone to write their names in large letters across a piece of paper, leaving some room around the edges.

   ✪ Now everyone can decorate their name using favourite colours, shapes and patterns.

   ✪ Draw a frame around the picture in a solid colour.

> **Sharing**   In small groups show others your name picture and compare your different styles and colours.

> **Ending**   Ask the group to say their name quietly to themselves in a positive tone of voice, and to use this to push away any thoughts of when people might have said it in an angry, sarcastic or bullying voice.

My Special Name

 Children  Teenagers

Aims To develop personal choices.

Materials Thick drawing paper or card, glitter-glue pens, thick felt-tip pens, tissue paper in different colours.

Warm Up Tell the group that they are going to think of a new name for themselves and then walk round the room thinking about whether they would behave differently with this new name; now introduce yourself to others with this new name.

Focus Choose a new name that you would really like to have (this could be in addition to the name you already have); it might be the same name you used in the warm-up or a different one.

Discussion In pairs, compare your own name with the new one, does a name make a difference to how you feel? Have you always wanted a different name? What are the reasons for people not liking their names?

Activities Using the glitter glue, write the new name that you would like to be known by on a piece paper or card.

- ⊗ Stick scrunched-up pieces of tissue paper in your favourite colour onto your name so that it really stands out.

- ⊗ Decorate the rest of the sheet of paper to create a picture.

- ⊗ Using the glitter glue or coloured pens to make a frame round the edges of the picture.

Sharing Now show and discuss the name picture with your partner, how does it feel to actually 'own' the new name?

Ending Create a display of all the new names on the wall. Ask people to see if they can guess who the names belong to.

Understanding Myself

29 Self-Portrait – this is ME!

☑ Children ☑ Teenagers

Aims To build self-esteem and individuality, and aspects of self-awareness.

Materials A3 thick paper, crayons, coloured pens, pencils, coloured tissue paper and white stick glue.

Warm Up Energise the group with age-appropriate running/jumping/dancing exercises such pretending to jump over hot coals, or dancing up and down with excitement. Play variations of follow 'Follow my Leader', or 'Simon Says' or 'Watch my Finger' (a pair game where one person sticks out a finger, and their partner has to stare at the finger and follow it round the room).

Focus With a partner, stand facing each other, and then take it in turns to pretend to look in a mirror; your partner is the mirror and must reflect any movement you make.

Discussion Had you ever really looked closely at your partner's face before? What did you notice? Do you remember what colour their eyes are?

Activities Working in pairs, lie down one at a time with head and shoulders on a piece of paper, while partners draw around the outline.

⊗ Now each person can colour in their own picture, try to create the correct hair and eye colours. Try to think about details of your appearance.

⊗ If people like they could add something to their heads such as a cap or a ballerina's bow or a cycle helmet, to show an activity they enjoy doing.

⊗ Try to make the portrait in three dimensions by using small pieces of tissue paper and glue them on for features.

Sharing Show each other your portrait and talk about how it feels to have created a picture of yourself; would someone in your family know that it was you?

Ending Write down three things that you really like and three things that you don't like doing.

This is My Hand

☑ Children ⚪ Teenagers

> **Aims** To affirm individual identity and difference.

> **Materials** A4 white paper, finger paints, coloured pencils and crayons, coloured pens, glitter glue, wet wipes.

Warm Up Suggest that everyone holds up their hands with the palms facing you, wiggle fingers, twist wrists, wave with one hand and then the other.

Focus Invite everyone to look closely at both of their hands, first the backs and then the palms; are they the same?

Discussion Is anyone left-handed? Can anyone use both hands?

Activities Draw round one hand on a sheet of paper with a pencil. Write your name inside your hand and then decorate the hand and fingers to make an individual portrait.

⊗ Use finger paints to make a hand print on a sheet of paper. Look at how everyone's hand is different in size and shape, can you see the pattern of lines?

⊗ Using finger paints, ask every group member to take turns to make a thumb print on a large sheet of paper. Discuss how everyone's thumb print is different.

> **Sharing** Talk about how everyone's hands are special and have their own individual features. Each person's hands look different from other people's and they can do different activities.

> **Ending** Complete the sentence: 'My hands are good at...

Understanding Myself

31 Freeze Frames

✓ Children ◯ Teenagers

Aims To strengthen positive body image and awareness of body language.

Materials Space large enough to run around, tambour or small drum.

Warm Up Encourage everyone to run around the room and to stop and freeze when you beat the drum. Repeat the exercise until everyone can listen for the beat and respond appropriately. You can vary this with skipping round the room or walking briskly.

Focus Ask everyone to walk around the room and then at the signal stop in a very proud or confident posture; next time, try stopping in a shy or nervous posture; then repeat the confident freeze frame.

Discussion How did it feel to be in one posture and then the other? In what ways did people's bodies feel different with the two postures? On what occasions do people walk in a positive way?

Activities Working with a partner, think of a situation where one person feels good about themselves and the other one doesn't; now create a short role-play without words, using freeze frames (body sculpts) to show the scene to the group, then swap roles and repeat it the performance.

Sharing How did it feel to be in each of the roles? Did anyone find any of the scenes familiar?

Ending Complete the sentences:

'I don't feel good about myself when...'
'I feel good about myself when...'

Understanding Myself

I am the Champion!

 Children  Teenagers

> **Aims** To encourage self-belief and affirmation of success.

> **Materials** Age-appropriate magazines and newspapers, scissors, glue stick, sheets of paper.

Warm Up Divide the group in half. One half then sings 'We are the champions' and the other half sings 'You are the champions' with the appropriate hand claps in between. Encourage the groups to change their voices from very loud to a quiet whisper, and then swap the groups round.

Focus Sitting with a partner, think of all the words that we use about people who are successful. Has anyone used these words about us?

Discussion Talk about words that describe success and whether they are important; is it more important to finish first or to finish well?

Activities Working individually, cut out words and sentences about success and doing well from magazines and newspapers. Make a collage by sticking them on a piece of paper, together with pictures.

⊗ Now create a success collage about a person that you admire, using pictures and words.

⊗ Write your name in the middle of a piece of paper and decorate it with different colours. Then surround it with words or phrases that you would like other people to say to you such as 'That's great' or 'Well done!'

> **Sharing** Do we all admire similar qualities in other people? How might these people feel in their private lives, even if they are successful in their public or work lives?

> **Ending** Complete these sentences:
>
> 'I would really like someone [who?] to notice that I am good at ...'
> 'If a friend has done well, I will try and notice and say ...'

Understanding Myself

33 My Idea Wall (i)

☑ Children ☑ Teenagers

Understanding Myself

Aims	To build a solid foundation for self-development.

Materials	Large white board and assorted coloured markers.

Warm Up   Physical stretch and shake; imagine there is a wall in front of you, stretch up to look over the top – it's too high; now stretch to look round the side – it's too wide; stretch up just a little more – you can just see over! Greet whoever you see there.

Focus   Invite everyone to think about how walls are built, and how they need strong and deep foundations.

Discussion   What makes us who we are? What give us a strong foundation in life? What qualities do we need for building our lives.

Activities   Using the white board, draw a row of bricks to form the beginning of the group's personal wall. Group members could each draw their own wall on a sheet of paper.

- ✪ Now think about words that describe what is needed to build a strong foundation together; which words do people feel apply to the foundations they already have.

- ✪ Write these words inside the bricks.

- ✪ Continue drawing bricks and building the wall, as people think of words to fill them.

- ✪ Create a separate pile of 'missing' bricks containing the words that the group would like to have in the wall as the sessions progress. How might these be achieved?

Sharing	Working with a partner discuss what you contributed to the wall and the pile of 'missing words' bricks – see if you have similar words.

Ending	Discuss in the whole group how everyone can work together to acquire the extra bricks.

My Idea Wall (ii)

 Children  Teenagers

---

Aims To practice the qualities and social skills needed to build a solid foundation for the future.

Materials Newspapers for standing on, pieces of card, felt-tipped pens; music and CD player.

Warm Up Play 'Newspaper Islands' – place sheets of newspaper round the room (fewer than there are group members); play the music, and when it stops everyone has to stand on the nearest sheet; several people might have to share one island – how can you all stay on? If you fall off the newspaper then you are out!

Focus Discuss with a partner whether you were able to hold everyone on the newspaper or were some people lost? How did it feel if you were one of the people who fell off an island and were out? Think of words to describe how it felt to work together to stay on the islands.

Discussion In the whole group discuss the words everyone came up with for the pile of 'missing bricks' in the previous exercise. Did some people have the same ideas, and are there groups of people who thought of similar words?

Activities Start with everyone working on their own 'bricks' before sharing with a partner.

- ⊗ Ask everyone to draw a brick on their piece of card, and write the most important word from your 'missing brick' ideas inside it.

- ⊗ Draw three more bricks around the outside of the first one and join the outer bricks to the centre one with a line.

- ⊗ Write words inside three new bricks which describe the help you might need to achieve your aim in the centre brick.

Sharing With a partner look at your brick diagrams and compare them, maybe you have something in common and can help each other?

Ending As a group, choose one word that that everyone connects with and think about how the group can all help each other.

Understanding Myself

35 My Idea Wall (iii)

☑ Children ☑ Teenagers

> **Aims** To encourage understanding and empathy.

> **Materials** Large sheets of paper/card; coloured pens and markers, white board.

Warm Up 'Blind walk'. In pairs, take it in turns to close your eyes and then be lead around the room by your partner, the seeing person must make sure their partner does not bump into anything or anyone else.

Focus Ask the group to call out, one at a time, words that people might write on their walls in order to give them a strong foundation, and write these clearly on the board.

Discussion As a group, think about which of the words need a lot of practice and which of them need a change of attitude?

Activities Ask each person to draw a wall on their sheet of paper that is five bricks long and three bricks high and write their name at the top of the page.

- ⊗ Now each person can write in the first row of bricks five qualities they feel they already have in their wall.
- ⊗ Swap sheets with someone else and now write on the next row five qualities that you feel your partner could add right now (use a different colour).
- ⊗ Now swap with another person who writes in the top row five qualities that your previous partner could achieve, but which will take time (use a different colour again).

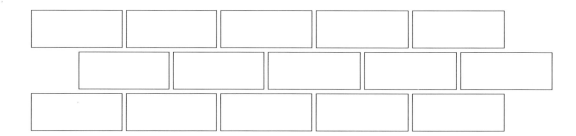

> **Sharing** Discuss with a partner your 'gifts' from other people; how do you feel about what people have written, are you disappointed that there are gifts you did not receive?

> **Ending** In the whole group discuss the most important gift you received today.

Understanding Myself

My Needs – Your Needs   36

✓ Children   ✓ Teenagers

> **Aims** To encourage recognition of the needs of others as well as your own.

> **Materials** Enough space for moving around, a variety of hats and caps, paper and pencils.

Warm Up Encourage everyone to move around the room in different ways: first striding; then tiptoeing; running in slow-motion; running fast. Now pretend to be pushing or elbowing other people out of the way as you walk, taking care not to touch anyone else. Put on a hat or a cap and walk in the character of the hat or cap.

Focus With a partner take turns to sit quietly and watch everything that is happening while the other person strides up and down the room without looking from side to side.

Discussion How different are the experiences of looking everywhere and only looking straight ahead of you?

Activities With a partner, talk about the things that you feel you need (rather than the things that you want).

- ✪ Maybe these are physical objects, but what about feelings?

- ✪ Do people need care? Affection? Control?

- ✪ How might you notice if someone needs something? Can you tell if someone needs care?

Write down the words you have explored together and decide which are the most important.

> **Sharing** What did people learn about their partners? Do they need care or someone to be a friend? Would you have guessed if they had not told you?

> **Ending** Draw a picture, or write a short description of someone who is your friend or someone you would like to be your friend. Write down the qualities they have that you like.

Understanding Myself

37 The 'Me' You See

☑ Children ☑ Teenagers

> **Aims** To encourage insight into how others see us.

> **Materials** Strong paper or card, coloured markers, crayons, coloured pens.

Warm Up Walk round the room and do 'high fives' with alternate hands with everyone you meet; repeat, but this time clap your hands in between the high fives.

Focus Find a partner and discuss one thing you really dislike about what people say about you.

Discussion Think about how easy it is to label other people. Is this because of assumptions we make about them or is it because of the way individuals actually behave?

Activities Think of the people in your life who know you: your mum, teacher, football coach, and create a shield or poster showing how these people see you.

✪ Now create a second shield or poster showing how people see you because of who or what you are: I'm black or I'm a teenager or I'm disabled.

✪ Put the two pictures side-by-side and see whether there are any links: for example, do people see me as being aggressive just because I am a teenager, or am I aggressive anyway, do the people who know me well also see this?

> **Sharing** Discuss with a partner whether you have ever been bullied and why you think it is: your looks, your race, your hobbies.

> **Ending** Ask everyone think about one thing other people might say about them, and write this down.

The 'Me' You Don't See

 Children Teenagers

Aims To encourage confidence in sharing difficult feelings.

Materials A4 white paper, crayons and coloured pens, white board and markers.

Warm Up First ask everyone to walk, then run, round the room, avoiding any eye contact with other people; then repeat with people looking at everyone as they move around; repeat a third time, but this time greet everyone you meet.

Focus Close your eyes and think about something you would like to share but do not feel confident that you can. (Be alert to the possibility that this exercise could trigger painful memories that could need some follow-up.)

Discussion Talk about the differences between those issues that are private and that we should not be expected to share, and those issues that really we need to tell someone about.

Activities Using the white board, ask the group for suggestions of general themes that people might be reluctant to share (rather than focussing on individuals and specific issues), for example: being bullied, mental health difficulties at home, parental breakup imminent, family member in prison.

- ✪ Ask group members to think about which situations they feel empathy towards, because they have experienced something similar themselves. Remind people that empathy is feeling how the other person feels, sympathy is feeling sorry for someone.

- ✪ What would make participants feel confident enough to own those feelings for themselves?

- ✪ Ask everyone to write down one event that would encourage them to show empathy towards someone else's situation.

Sharing Talk with a partner about the sorts of things that are difficult to share and why that might be: maybe it would result in bullying or feeling disloyal to your family?

Ending Complete the following sentences:

Children can be frightened to talk about...
Teenagers often keep quiet about...

Understanding Myself

39 I was Trying to Say...

⬭ Children   ☑ Teenagers

Understanding Myself

> **Aims** To help teenagers to express stored-up resentments.

> **Materials** A variety of hats including uniform caps/helmets, sets of hand-cuffs.

Warm Up Move around the room and imagine you are running across the park, hood pulled down over your face and not looking at anyone else. Without looking at anyone else, pause and shout 'Where?', continue running, pause and shout 'Here!', run and pause 'When?', pause and shout 'Now!'.

Focus Using the phrase 'If only...' create your own chant with hand clap.

Discussion Why can it be so difficult to say the things we need to say? How can we make sure we create a space in order to have our say?

Activities Using the props and hats, create an authoritarian scene which develops the theme of creating the space to say something:

- ✪ Divide into groups of three: one person is the authority figure, one is trying to explain something and third person keeps interrupting and not letting them finish.

- ✪ Take it in turns to play all the roles.

- ✪ Examples: explain to a policeman that it was not you who broke the window or to a teacher the reason for being late.

- ✪ Stay in the groups of three, choose two people to stay silent while the third starts to speak, 'What I am trying to explain is…' Take it in turns to be this person.

> **Sharing** In small groups of three discuss which of the roles was the most difficult to play. Has anyone had a similar experience in real life they could talk about?

> **Ending** Have a whole group discussion on the theme of finding ways of saying what we need to say: who can be the most difficult people to talk to?

I'm in Charge

 Children  Teenagers

Aims To empower individuals and encourage leadership.

Materials None.

Warm Up March on the spot, making sure you are standing tall; take it in turns to play 'Follow My Leader', where everyone follows and copies the leader who is marching round the room.

Focus Close your eyes and think about the qualities you respect in leadership.

Discussion With a partner or in a small group discuss your ideas and find out if you admire similar qualities in leaders. Who has the role of leader in your family?

Activities In small groups of three or four, experiment with different leadership styles in different contexts (e.g., the classroom, the playground, in a shop).

⊗ One person volunteers to 'be in charge' and tests out different styles of leadership:

- Ordering people to do something.

- Inviting people to do something.

- Suggesting people do something.

⊗ Make sure that everyone has the chance to play role of leader and change the context each time to avoid repetition.

Sharing Which style do people find the most comfortable when they are leader and which is most comfortable when they are followers? Are there times when you have to be more authoritarian?

Ending Observe and discuss what you see in the different body postures when people change leadership styles. Be aware of your own gestures when giving instructions.

Understanding Myself

Part Three
Building Awareness & Confidence

Themes

41　I Can't Hear You!

 Children　 Teenagers

Aims　To encourage exploration of differences in people's voices.

Materials　Sheets of paper or card and coloured markers.

Warm Up　Encourage everyone to explore 'body percussion' and beat rhythms on their legs, chests, cheeks, hands and feet.

Focus　Continue the percussion with vocal sounds – ask the group to call out sounds from the forest, the farm, the city – any sound that comes to mind, and to make the sounds loud and soft, shouted or whispered.

Discussion　Ask group members about people whose voices they will always listen to, what are the qualities of these voices?

Activities　Ask the group to write about or draw the following:

⊗ A person whose voice you found you could not listen to;

⊗ A person whose voice you did not notice, it was just in the background;

⊗ A person who you listened to with pleasure.

Sharing　Explore with partners or in small groups these three types of voice and the people they belonged to; discuss any connections with voices of people in the past and voices in the present. For example, perhaps there is a connection between the sound of a voice you did not like in the past and your reaction to someone in the present or possibly you are drawn towards someone now, who happens to have a voice of someone in the past.

Ending　Invite group members to look at the ideas on their cards and write down the qualities they would like to have in their own voices.

Building Awareness & Confidence

Speak Up!

 ✓ Children ✓ Teenagers

Aims To gradually build confidence in order to be able to speak to others in an empathic way.

Materials Card, paper and coloured markers.

Warm Up Suggest everyone moves around the room at a fast walks, one after the other call out different styles of walking: very tall, very small, very tired, very energetic. Now imagine you are running after an escaped pet, try to catch it and take it home again.

Focus Ask the group to continue this theme working in pairs, and talk about the imaginary pet they have just chased and caught. (What is it? What happened? How did it feel?) Try to use as many words as possible to describe the pet and your feelings at having caught it; partners can ask questions to draw out the story.

Discussion Find out from the group members whether anyone owns a pet or would like to have one, and what sort of animal they might feel close to?

Activities Invite everyone to either write a description or draw a picture of a pet that they own or would like to own (if anyone doesn't want a pet, ask them to describe something else that they would really like to own):

❸ Each person has one minute to tell the group about their pet.

❸ Follow this with group members asking each other questions about their pets.

Sharing Divide into pairs and discuss any new words people have thought of to describe their pet.

Ending Explore in the whole group about any difficulties people may encounter when speaking in public.

Building Awareness & Confidence

43 Hey You!

◯ Children ✓ Teenagers

Aims To encourage teenagers to respond rather than react, and to understand that sometimes people react to the way they are spoken to rather than the content of the words.

Materials Card and coloured markers; football in case additional ice-breaking games are needed.

Warm Up Encourage the group to choose their own game(s) for the warm up.

Focus Ask the group to walk briskly round the room, in and out of each other, then call 'Freeze!', everyone must stand perfectly still until you start them off again. Vary the freeze by calling out a style to freeze in: e.g., hiding from your mates because you are playing a joke on them; hiding from a teacher because you think you are in trouble.

Discussion Explore how people would react differently depending on who they were freezing or stopping for, including those in authority.

Activities Invite the group to form pairs and write down a joint list of things that annoy them about the way adults communicate: forgetting young people's names; embarrassing them in front of other people; shouting:

✪ Each pair creates and shows a freeze frame to the whole group of an example from their discussion.

✪ Each pair demonstrates how they would like to be spoken to by the adult from their freeze frame.

Sharing Suggest group members share with their partner how they feel inside when an adult speaks to them in the 'wrong' way.

Ending Discuss in the whole group whether anyone has caused others to 'react' by using phrases or words that have embarrassed them.

Please Listen! (i)

☑ Children   ☑ Teenagers

Aims To understand the differences between wants and needs.

Materials Large piece of card for each person and assorted coloured markers.

Warm Up Ask group members to choose a partner and play 'pretend hopscotch' or another game (see Introduction).

Focus With partners, discuss the differences between the following statements: 'What do I want most?' and 'What do I really need?'.

Discussion Bring the whole group together and explore the different ideas people have discussed in their pairs.

Activities Ensure each group member has a piece of card and coloured pens.

- ✪ Divide the card into 4 equal parts and number them 1 to 4.

- ✪ In square 1, write or draw something that you really want.

- ✪ In square 2, write or draw something you really need.

- ✪ In square 3, write or draw how you will get the thing you want.

- ✪ In square 4, write or draw who will give you the things you need.

Sharing With a partner compare what you have written in the squares and discuss any similarities and differences.

Ending Relax back-to-back with your partner and think about the difference between your wants and needs.

Building Awareness & Confidence

45 Please Listen! (ii)

 Children Teenagers

Aims Further understanding of needs and wants.

Materials CD Player and CD of 'All You Need is Love' (The Beatles) or other music that reflects a similar theme and is age-appropriate. A sheet containing the lyrics to the song, for reference. White board and markers. Sheets of card, newspapers and magazines, scissors and glue.

Warm Up Invite members of the group to walk round the room and listen to the lyrics, and really hear the words.

Focus Suggest that everyone finds a partner and together think of as many songs, poems, films as they can that are about needing or wanting love or losing love.

Discussion Invite the whole group to think of as many different ways that we can love; for example we love our pet in one way and we love our little brother or sister in another, and write them on the white board.

Activities Ask everyone to create their own poem on the theme of 'Love':

⊗ Write the title 'Something about Love' on the white board for everyone to copy;

⊗ Using newspapers and magazines, cut out words and phrases that fit the title of the poem;

⊗ Stick these on a piece of card to create a poem and decorate it with coloured pens.

Sharing Suggest that everyone works with their original partner and shares their poem by showing their artwork to them. (At this stage, reading the poem could make people feel too vulnerable.)

Ending Allow everyone to sit wrapped in their blanket and listen to the music again, or share with the whole group something they have learned today. (Choose your own ending depending on the age of the group and how vulnerable people appear to be.)

Building Awareness & Confidence

Please Listen! (iii)

◯ Children   ☑ Teenagers

Aims   To create an awareness of how love can be used for bribery and blame.

Materials   Large whiteboard – double size if possible – plenty of coloured markers.

Warm Up   Invite group members to physically 'shake out' or run on the spot. Then choose a partner, hold hands and experiment with allowing your partner to pull you easily around the room, and then trying to stay firm and resist being pulled; then change round.

Focus   Explore with your partner whether you found it more difficult to 'let go' or to 'stay firm'.

Discussion   Continue to explore these themes with the whole group and introduce the phrases 'If you really loved me you would...' and 'If you really love me you wouldn't have ...', and ask if anyone has very heard these used.

Activities   Write the two phrases on the board and then encourage group members to contribute suggestions to complete the sentences:

- ✪ Write all the phrases on the board, e.g., 'If you really loved me you would stay in at night'.

- ✪ Colour code the responses, e.g., red for things parents/carers might say, green for boy or girl friends, blue for anyone else.

- ✪ Ask group members to underline the phrases familiar to them with the appropriate colour for their situation, e.g., the above phrase might be said by a parent or a girlfriend.

Sharing   Explore in the whole group whether love should ever be used to bribe or blame.

Ending   Invite people to share with a partner situations where they have used love in this way with someone else.

Building Awareness & Confidence

47 Please Listen! (iv)

✓ Children   ◯ Teenagers

Aims To help understand how people can be persuaded to do things and to learn the difference between emotional blackmail and being talked into things you just don't want to do.

Materials Large white board and coloured markers.

Warm Up Ask the group to move around the room, imagining they are walking a dog on a lead and that sometimes the dog pulls them very strongly and they have to run, and sometimes it tugs just a little, they can be pulled backwards and forwards!

Focus Form pairs and ask everyone to talk with their partner about times when they feel 'pushed' to do something.

Discussion Explore in the whole group the sort of things people feel pushed to do by others, and the methods used by other people to persuade them to do something that is inappropriate.

Activities Continue to explore in the whole group the idea of being persuaded to do something:

- ⊗ Write on the board. 'You must do this because I love you'; or, especially with children, 'You must do this because I am your friend';

- ⊗ Ask group members to suggest what 'this' could be and write responses on board;

- ⊗ Now ask for suggestions of who might be saying this, and write responses on board.

Sharing Suggest that everyone talks in pairs about their own feelings at times when they have been persuaded to do things that they did not want to do. How could they respond if this happens again? Are there are other ways to persuade people?

Ending Invite everyone to make a circle, stamp their feet 1, 2, 3, clap their hands 1, 2, 3 and beat their chests 1, 2, 3. Repeat several times.

Too Much, Too Little (i) 48

☑ Children ○ Teenagers

Aims To consider how our feelings can be overwhelmed or underwhelmed.

Materials Fleecy blanket for each person, long ribbons or scarves, CDs of rhythmic music for dancing, and calm music for relaxing, CD player, Worksheet 3.

Warm Up Tell the group that to start with they must stand as far away from everyone else as possible and then stand as close together as they can to make the smallest group possible; repeat the exercise first by changing group size very slowly, and then very quickly.

Focus Invite everyone to stand in the room at the distance from others that feels comfortable for them.

Discussion Suggest that people tell a partner what it feels like to have others too close or too far away. Try to name the feelings such as 'I feel scared or it makes me nervous or I get anxious when you stand so close to me' or 'I feel lost or I panic when you are so far away'. (See also Worksheet 3.)

Activities Ask people to move into the space with a partner and one scarf each and suggest that they:

⊗ Make shapes and patterns with the scarves, standing a comfortable space apart;

⊗ Hold the ends of both scarves and make shapes and see if the distance feels comfortable; is it the same for both of you?

⊗ Dance or move to the music with your partner, each making patterns with scarves and feeling comfortable about the space between.

Sharing Suggest that everyone shares in the whole group whether they felt secure in the group today.

Ending Curl up in fleecy blankets and listen to calming music.

49 Too Much, Too Little (ii)

◯ Children ☑ Teenagers

> **Aims** To encourage insight into different types of personal spaces, who inhabits them and what makes people comfortable in them.

> **Materials** Pieces of card with concentric circles drawn on them; coloured markers and pens; Worksheet 3.

Warm Up Ask the group to form pairs and facing each other, negotiate a distance between them that feels comfortable. Now one person should put their hand up, palm towards their partner and slowly move towards them and then back again; when does it feel uncomfortable or 'in your face'? Change over.

Focus Suggest that everyone explores with their partner times when they say 'Just back off' or 'Hey, not so close' – is it to friends, family or other people?

Discussion Talk in the whole group about the different types of spaces and the words to describe them. Who makes you feel uncomfortable by being too close?

Activities Give each person a copy of Worksheet 3, this can also be drawn on the board, explain that the inner circle represents personal space, then private space, social space, public space and open space.

⊗ Ask the group to label, name and colour each circle and think about who inhabits or is allowed into each space.

⊗ Around the edges of the circles write anything you want to say about the different spaces.

⊗ Are there any spaces that others come into when they are not wanted? In particular does your personal space ever feel invaded?

> **Sharing** Suggest that everyone works with their original partner and compares the spaces that they find OK and those that are difficult.

> **Ending** In the whole group, invite everyone to make suggestions about how they might feel more comfortable about their personal space.

Building Awareness & Confidence

Too Much, Too Little (iii) 50

○ Children ☑ Teenagers

> **Aims** To explore ways of managing people who are 'too close'.

> **Materials** A variety of hats, scarves and caps.

Warm Up Suggest each person takes a hat, scarf or cap and walks around the room as if they are the person wearing it: no words, only walking, posture and gestures; change hats at least three times.

Focus Choose one hat to represent someone in real life who you feel is sometimes too close and discuss this with a partner.

Discussion In the whole group discuss situations where people are too close and which can be difficult to handle.

Activities Invite people to form small groups of three and think of a scene to role-play:

✪ Choose a scene that shows a negative way of handling someone being too close (such as pushing someone away);

✪ Show your scene to the whole group using only freeze frames and no speech;

✪ Repeat, but this time show another way of handling the situation that is more positive.

> **Sharing** Ask people to comment on which of the scenes they recognised from their own experience, and what they thought about the solutions shown.

> **Ending** Discuss in small groups how it felt to play roles, and which one would they like to play on another occasion.

Building Awareness & Confidence

51 Scary Places (i)

☑ Children ◯ Teenagers

> **Aims** To enable expression of fears and anxieties about places that feel unsafe.

> **Materials** Drawing paper and coloured pens and markers.

Warm Up Suggest that everyone moves around the room, first 'walking tall' and then 'walking small'; then take tiny footsteps followed by big strides.

Focus In the whole group, or in pairs, talk about scary things and spaces: these could be TV programmes, videos, places in the house, at school or outside.

Discussion Continue the discussion with partner or in the whole group about what happens to our bodies when we are scared or feel anxious: where do we feel it? Maybe in stomachs, mouths or necks? What happens to our heart beat?

Activities Invite group members to think about all the things they have discussed with their partner and choose one to explore in more detail.

⊗ Draw a picture of the 'scary place' and think about the atmosphere there.

⊗ Put yourself in the picture, whereabouts are you?

⊗ Does the drawing create the feelings of anxiety again?

> **Sharing** Discuss in the whole group whether thinking about a scary place is more or less scary than actually being there? Allow for as much variation as possible.

> **Ending** Share with the same partner whether feelings can be changed by telling somebody else. What fears would we like change most?

Scary Places (ii)

 ◯ Children ✓ Teenagers

---

Aims To enable understanding of the difference between feelings and emotions.

Materials Coloured pens and white board. (Optional: notes on the basic brain structure from Gibb, *The Rough Guide to the Brain* or Pinel & Edwards, *A Colourful Introduction to the Anatomy of the Human Brain*; see Useful Reading.)

Warm Up Ask everyone to walk round the room and to freeze in an appropriate body shape when one of the following is called: athlete, biker, footballer, swimmer, boxer; surprised, angry, scared, cool, bored.

Focus Form small groups of three or four and discuss the differences in feelings and emotions experienced in the different freezes in the warm up.

Discussion Explain the difference between feelings and emotions: emotions are expressed spontaneously through the body (usually triggered by the amygdala part of the brain) when there is an emotional stimulus or memory: pounding heart, sweaty palms, blushing for example; write headings on the board if necessary. A feeling is what the higher brain constructs to explain the emotions. Open a whole-group discussion by sharing the emotions that make us feel uncomfortable.

Activities Invite members of the group to remember an incident in the past that made them feel very angry.

 ✪ Close your eyes and bring the memory into the present.

 ✪ Be aware of any bodily changes such as increase in your heart beat, muscle tension perhaps in your hands and face.

 ✪ Breathe deeply and leave the memory, and think of something you enjoy doing.

Sharing With a partner, tell the story of the specific event that triggered the emotions.

Ending Share with the partner what you may have learned about your own emotions.

Building Awareness & Confidence

53 Scary Places (iii)

 Children Teenagers

Aims	To encourage recognition of feelings and to own them.

Materials	Selection of magazines and newspapers, card, scissors and glue, Worksheet 4.

Warm Up General physical shake-out; walk round the room, run round the room.

Focus Suggest that everyone runs around the room, first, as if they are late to meet a friend; then as if they are running away from something scary; then, as if they will be told off for being late; finally, as if something very special is about to happen.

Discussion Invite everyone to discuss in the whole group how their running differed depending on the reason. What were the physical differences and how do these relate to emotions being portrayed? (See Worksheet 4.)

Activities Suggest that everyone works with a partner to create a collage of feelings:

⊗ Choose one feeling (e.g., pleasure, fear, anger) and cut out pictures of people who show that feeling.

⊗ Stick them on the card and colour any spaces in between, so it becomes a total picture.

Sharing	Show the collage pictures in the whole group and think about variations between the expressions on the different people.

Ending	With a partner talk about a situation where the feeling shown in your collage was strong.

Building Awareness & Confidence

I'm Tough

✓ Children ✓ Teenagers

Aims To increase awareness of feeling tough and how others might feel about this.

Materials Coloured sticky tape and scissors.

Warm Up General shake-out; everyone moves about as if they are boxing (no touching of other people is allowed); now move about like someone who is in the boxing ring but does not want to fight.

Focus Suggest that everyone works with a partner and takes turns to stand tall and pose as the tough person while their partner poses as a scared person; then change over.

Discussion Invite discussion around the topic of whether we need someone else to be weak in order for us to feel strong; what happens when two tough or two scared people get together?

Activities Ask the group to line up in rows facing their partners, use two strips of the coloured tape to mark out a 'no go' area between the rows: for volatile groups this may need to be quite wide.

- ✪ Working with a partner, 'shadow-box' keeping behind the lines and making sure there is no touching.

- ✪ Create the idea of two celebrities who are going to shadow-box, and enter the space in imaginary costumes, bowing to the crowds and so on (remember to leave enough time for everyone to come out of role at the end). Assuming another persona will create sufficient distance for participants to feel less foolish – many teenagers will have enormous difficulty doing this as themselves or just anyone.

Sharing Invite everyone to tell the whole group how it felt to be the celebrity boxing in front of the audience.

Ending Everyone closes their eyes, sits calmly and practises deep and calming breathing.

 ℗ This page may be photocopied for instructional use only. *101 Activities for Empathy & Awareness* © Sue Jennings 2011

Building Awareness & Confidence

55   I Can Cope (i)

 ☑ Children ☑ Teenagers

> **Aims**   To help people to understand that 'coping' is not necessarily the best solution.

> **Materials**   Large white board and coloured markers.

Warm Up   Ask the group to walk around the room; as they walk each person turns away from others, avoids eye contact, and says quietly 'I am fine'; then repeat the walking and quietly say 'I am not fine'; repeat, this time shouting 'I am fine!' and again 'I am not fine!'.

Focus   Suggest that everyone thinks about what we mean when we say we are coping; make use of the board and markers and allow people to write down words and feelings about coping.

Discussion   Start the discussion by suggesting that there are many situations where people have to cope: e.g., with parents who are ill; having a sibling with special needs; with school work that we do not understand.

Activities   Invite the group to stand in a large circle.

⊗ Start with one person turning to the person on their right and saying 'I can cope' and that person responds by saying 'I can't cope'; then they turn and say to the person on their right 'I can cope', and receive the response 'I can't cope'; the phrase and response go all the way round the group.

⊗ Repeat the exercise starting with 'I'm feeling fine' and the response 'I feel terrible'.

> **Sharing**   Continue in the whole group, sharing how it felt to say you could not cope or did not feel fine.

> **Ending**   Invite everyone to sit with a partner and complete the following phrases 'I can cope with... but I can't cope with...' or 'I am fine when...but I am not fine when...'

I Can Cope (ii)

 Children  Teenagers

> **Aims** To encourage the group to acknowledge that it is OK to tell someone if they are struggling for some reason and cannot cope.

> **Materials** Large white board and coloured markers; plain card, scissors and coloured pens.

Warm Up Explain that the group will take it in turns to call out 'Everyone's invited to my party!' and the group responds by shouting out 'Great!', 'Thanks!', etc. Repeat the invitation with everyone responding by shouting out, for example, 'Sorry, can't come!', 'Got stuff going on at home!'.

Focus Suggest that everyone works with a partner and shares something they would like to do but they can't because of 'stuff going on at home'.

Discussion Make use of the white board and markers to identify what the 'stuff going on at home' might be. For example, a relative there may be ill and needs to be looked after, or someone may be struggling with their schoolwork and needs to spend extra time studying.

Activities Find ways of developing the focus of caring for someone else (e.g., younger sibling, sick mother, alcohol-dependant father); give everyone some card and coloured pens and markers.

⊗ Ask everyone to draw two masks, one of the person who does the caring, and the other of the person being cared for, and then cut them out.

⊗ Working with a partner, hold up the mask of the carer and say 'When I am caring for someone I feel...' and their partner holds up their cared-for mask, and says, 'When I am cared-for I feel...'. Change over.

⊗ Repeat the exercise but this time the person wearing the cared-for mask says, 'When I am cared for I need...' and the partner replies, wearing their carer mask, 'When I am caring I will give you...'

> **Sharing** Invite everyone to share in the whole group how it felt to speak wearing the cared-for mask.

> **Ending** Encourage everyone to write on the back of their carer mask why they would also like to be cared for.

 Ⓟ This page may be photocopied for instructional use only. *101 Activities for Empathy & Awareness* © Sue Jennings 2011

Building Awareness & Confidence

57 You Just Don't Get It! (i)

⬭ Children ☑ Teenagers

Aims To allow time and space for young people to voice how they feel misunderstood by adults.

Materials Large white board, coloured markers, newspapers, card, scissors and glue.

Warm Up Invite everyone to move to a rap rhythm as they chant 'You just don't get it, you never will, I just get on with it 'coz you never will'.

Focus In pairs, invite everyone to tell their partners about adults who do not understand or who do not listen to what they are trying to say.

Discussion In the whole group ask people to speak from their partner's point of view and explain how they feel they are misunderstood.

Activities Continue the theme through simple role-play in groups of three and suggest the following scene:

⊗ A pupil is trying to tell something to a teacher who is not listening or attending (the third person stands to one side and voices what both characters are really are thinking during the conversation).

⊗ Give everyone the chance to play each role.

⊗ Ask for volunteers to role-play how this scene should ideally happen.

Sharing Ask people in the group if they identified with the scenes. Are the extra voices helpful (and/or truthful)?

Ending In pairs, think about what you feel you could do differently in order to be heard.

You Just Don't Get It! (ii)

☑ Children ◯ Teenagers

Aims To explore ways for children to tell an adult something important.

Materials Large white board and coloured markers, card and pens.

Warm Up Invite everyone to stand in a circle, clap a rhythm and call out together: 'Can't tell, won't tell', getting louder then softer; repeat with the phrase: 'Can tell, will tell', again getting louder and softer.

Focus With a partner, one person says 'I want to tell you something' and the other replies 'I'm busy'; repeat with both getting louder and louder and then change round.

Discussion Making use of the white board and markers, encourage everyone to suggest the sort of things they might like to tell an adult and write them down.

Activities Invite everyone to try and think of ways to get someone to listen to them.

- ✪ Using the card and pens, write a short letter to an adult asking them to listen to something important; it can explain what the 'important something' actually is, or can simply request some time with the adult.

- ✪ Read your letter out loud to a partner and listen to their letter.

- ✪ With your partner think of another person you could speak to: maybe they could explain to the adult that you need to tell them something.

Sharing Suggest that everyone practises saying the phrase 'I need to tell you something...' to different people.

Ending In the whole group, discuss trying out these ideas with different people and seeing what happens.

Building Awareness & Confidence

59 My Voice, My Words (i)

☑ Children　◯ Teenagers

Aims　To acknowledge that children need support to use their voices and be heard.

Materials　A variety of scarves, hats, caps.

Warm Up　Invite everyone to choose a scarf, hat or cap and walk around the room and then dance round the room.

Focus　Build on the theme of the previous activity by asking the whole group to stand in a circle and shout the phrase, 'I have something important to say!'.

Discussion　Think about who listens to us when we have something we need to say. One of our parents? A teacher? A grandparent or other relative? A friend?

Activities　Divide into groups of three, and number each person 1, 2 or 3; all the1s are the individual who needs to say something, all the 2s are the adult they need to speak to and the 3s are the guides who will help to coach the others (if the group does not divide, form pairs and then select a group to be guides).

✘ Decide who will be the listening adult (2s) and who needs to say something (1s) (use the hat props to help if wanted); the guides should then move round the pairs and point out when the listener is not listening or when the speaker is shouting or is not being heard.

✘ Give everyone the chance to play each role, and therefore the chance to be helped to be really heard.

Sharing　Discuss in the whole group how it felt to be heard, maybe for the first time, and how it felt to listen to other people's stories?

Ending　Suggest that everyone talks with their partner about how they can try out what they have learned in today's session.

My Voice, My Words (ii) 60

> **Aims** To help both individuals and groups to articulate their needs in an appropriate way.

> **Materials** Sheets of card and coloured markers.

Warm Up Shake-out and walk briskly round the room; and then run and on the signal make the shape of someone shouting; repeat with a different shape.

Focus Invite everyone to work with a partner and decide an important topic that needs to be heard.

Discussion Discuss in the whole group the sort of voices that are listened to and heard.

Activities Explain that everyone should work with their partner to create a short speech about their important topic:

 ✪ Write down the main points each pair wish to make in their speech; emphasise that they should keep the points very simple and focussed.

 ✪ Each pair now takes it in turns to read their speech to the group, either one at a time or together reading alternate sentences.

 ✪ The rest of the group must now give constructive feedback about tone of voice, posture, simplicity of points made and speech length.

> **Sharing** Encourage the pairs to comment on how it felt to have everyone listening to them. Did they agree with the feedback about their speech?

> **Ending** Continue the discussion in pairs, and think about how they might change their speech on another occasion.

Building Awareness & Confidence

Part Four
Accepting & Offering Support

Themes

61 Time Line (i)

☑ Children ☑ Teenagers

> **Aims** To increase awareness of the relationship between the past and life in the present.

> **Materials** Thick paper or card, crayons, coloured pens, white board and markers; or Worksheet 5.

Warm Up Think of circus activities, such 'walking a tightrope', or 'jumping through hoops' and invite group members to portray these actions with a partner.

Focus Think about the physical feeling of being off-balance and the idea of repeating the same thing over again.

Discussion In the whole group, discuss whether people feel burdened by their pasts, or do they forget about or even bury them? Write the different ideas on the board. Encourage the use of descriptive words such as dark and light, being in a forest or a desert, and so on.

Activities Using card or thick paper, or use Worksheet 5, and invite everyone in the group to draw a line or a road to represent their life until now, and mark any significant events along the way; what sort of landscape does this road pass through? Are there any stopping places?

> **Sharing** In pairs, suggest that the group share their pictures and talk about one significant event that has happened along the way.

> **Ending** In the whole group, invite everyone to talk about any aspects of their past they feel get in the way of moving forward.

Accepting & Offering Support

Time Line (ii)

☑ Children ◯ Teenagers

> **Aims** To encourage children to find symbolic ways of looking at their lives in the present and how they might unravel the different strands.

> **Materials** A4 pieces of card, glue sticks, piles of different coloured lengths of wool (approx 45cm/18 inches long) enough for each child, Worksheet 5.

Warm Up Invite everyone to stand in a circle, hold hands, and then start to weave over and under each other's arms until the group makes a knot; then try to untie the knot without breaking hands. This might have to be practised several times in order to stay joined together.

Focus Suggest in pairs, everyone explores the concept of 'knots'; for example, the sayings 'Get knotted!' or 'My stomach is in knots'.

Discussion How does it feel when there are things in our lives that we do not understand or that feel confusing or messy?

Activities Give each child a mixed up ball of the wool lengths, and suggest that this represents all the things that are muddling in their lives.

- ✪ Think about what each piece could represent (discard any that are not needed).

- ✪ See if they can be separated out as individual lengths.

- ✪ Now create a pattern with the wool of how you would like your life to look.

- ✪ Using the glue, stick your pattern on to the card.

> **Sharing** Working with your 'knots partner' share pictures and discuss their similarities and differences.

> **Ending** In the whole group, share anything that has become more clear through the creation of the unravelled life picture.

Accepting & Offering Support

63 Time Line (iii)

◯ Children   ☑ Teenagers

Aims To encourage young people to be more aware of different aspects of their lives and how they feel about them.

Materials Large quantity of coloured markers, A4 sheets of card, white board and markers, small pieces of paper and pens, Worksheet 5.

Warm Up Ask everyone to write on a piece of paper any question they would like to have answered or a statement about how they are feeling; ask everyone to read out their question or statement at the same time. Encourage people to read very loudly, then very quietly and then at an in-between volume, discovering that they cannot hear anyone else. Or maybe there is one voice you can hear?

Focus Ask for suggestions to complete the sentence 'Life is...' and write the ideas on the board. Underline any ideas that occur more than once.

Discussion Elaborate what is written on the board in a discussion about how we see our own lives, and what sort of words would be use to describe it. (See also Worksheet 5.)

Activities Invite everyone to select up to six coloured pens and two pieces of card.

⊗ Hold all the pens in one hand and draw round and round to make a messy circle or ball.

⊗ Think about how this could represent your life or an aspect of your life.

⊗ Use the second piece of card to create the separate threads or strands of your life using the individual colours.

⊗ Compare the two pictures, side by side.

Sharing With a partner, share the two pictures and talk about how 'separating out' can help people see things more clearly.

Ending Create two floor pictures: invite everyone to put their 'messy' pictures together to form a large collage and do the same with the second picture.

Accepting & Offering Support

Time Line (iv)

 Children  Teenagers

> **Aims** To help young people to think about the future and consider possible choices.

> **Materials** Long pieces of string; A4 card and coloured pens, white board and markers, Worksheet 5.

Warm Up Invite people to form groups of three where each person represents either the past, the present or the future; the past and the future must try to pull the third – present - person towards them, while they try to stay firmly planted in the present. Everyone should have a turn at the different roles.

Focus Stay in the threes, and take it in turns for 'Future' and 'Past' to call out a reason for the present to move either forwards and backwards; for example: 'Future' might call out 'Move on, it's fun here with friends!'; 'Past' might call out 'Move back here, you know it well, so life won't be scary'. 'Present' should call out that they are not going to move either way.

Discussion Suggest that everyone contributes to a discussion about how it feels to be caught between being pulled back and moving forwards. (See also Worksheet 5.)

Activities Working with a partner, suggest that everyone uses the string:

- ⊗ To create three obstacles that to represent things that might stop people moving forwards in their lives.

- ⊗ Then step over each 'barrier' and name it, for example: 'I have stepped over my struggles with literacy...'

- ⊗ Repeat the exercise but this time think of something to help overcome the barrier, for example, 'I have asked for help with my literacy so I will be able to move forward...'

> **Sharing** Now form pairs with a new partner and discuss and each write down on a piece of card the order in which their obstacles need to be removed. For example if someone is still excluded from school, it will be difficult to improve their literacy.

> **Ending** Invite everyone back to the whole group and write the most difficult obstacles on the white board; allow time for everyone to make suggestions for how these difficulties could be addressed.

Accepting & Offering Support

65 Asking for Help (i)

☑ Children ☑ Teenagers

> **Aims** To explore the idea of asking for and accepting help from another person.

> **Materials** White board and markers.

Warm Up Invite everyone to scatter round the room and find a place where they do not touch or crowd anyone else; at a handclap or drum beat, everyone should walk briskly around the room not touching or looking at anyone; repeat, but this time everyone should make eye contact, wave, high five or touch others on the shoulder.

Focus Discuss the idea of a continuum of trust and name one end, 'I don't trust anyone' and the other end 'I trust everybody' and imagine this line within the room. Now invite everyone to place themselves on the line where they think they are; repeat and ask them to move to where they would like to be on the line: less or more trusting?

Discussion In the whole group, invite participants to share how they felt about placing themselves on the continuum.

Activities Introduce the idea of a group sculpt, where the whole group are connected around a theme. Explore the following and place your hand on the shoulder of the person who you would trust to:

⊗ Lead you safely through a thick forest;

⊗ Light a fire for keeping warm and cooking;

⊗ Hold the end of the rope if you are climbing a cliff;

⊗ Work out your spending so you can save for something you really want.

⊗ There are lots more ideas you can add. However, be alert and ensure that everyone is chosen for at least one thing, or make sure that there are several people who do not get chosen.

> **Sharing** Invite everyone to share with a partner those things that they felt disappointed about not being chosen for.

> **Ending** Whole group discussion of how difficult it can be to trust other people.

Asking for Help (ii)

 Children Teenagers

> **Aims** To explore making simple requests for assistance without losing face.

> **Materials** Large white board, and sheets of card, markers.

Warm Up In threes, stand in a line, the two outside people must help the person in the middle person to jump higher and higher. Change over so everyone has a turn.

Focus Ask everyone to form pairs and talk about the most difficult thing they have ever asked for help with.

Discussion Invite the whole group to contribute ideas of difficulties they might ask help for, and write them on the large white board.

Activities Set up some role-play situations based on the ideas written on the white board, try to keep these at a light level. In these situations vary the format as follows:

✪ One person asks for help and the other person is unhelpful.

✪ Another person asks for help and the help is grudgingly given.

✪ Someone asks for help and it is given willingly.

✪ Why were some people willing to help and not others? Is it to do with the way the person asked? The mood of the person listening? The relationship between the two people?

> **Sharing** With the same partner, prepare a role-play where someone asks appropriately for help and it is given, then share the role-play with the whole group.

> **Ending** Write down on a sheet of card three things that are useful to remember when asking for help: for example, to explain why we need to know something; to address someone by their name; to acknowledge that we might be interrupting someone.

Accepting & Offering Support

67 Offering Help (i)

 Children  Teenagers

Aims To increase awareness of other people's interests and feelings, and begin to develop empathy.

Materials Age-appropriate magazines and newspapers; scissors, glue sticks, A4 card, coloured pens.

Warm Up Choose headlines from the newspapers that are very dramatic and create body sculpts in pairs, exaggerating gestures and facial expressions. Suggest that people try to guess what the headline might be.

Focus With the same partner choose one headline or story that would appeal an older person or to a granny.

Discussion Share all the 'granny' stories in the whole group and talk about why these events could appeal to older people.

Activities Invite everyone to choose headlines or stories from the newspapers and magazines that would come under the following headings:

⊗ A story that is really shocking.

⊗ A story that is really scary.

⊗ A story that is really sad.

⊗ Cut these out and stick them onto the card, use the coloured pens to decorate around them.

⊗ Think about what sort of people would respond to these stories; i.e., who would be shocked, scared or sad? Write your ideas around the pictures.

Sharing Share your card with a partner and discuss what you have written; see if they feel the same about how people might feel.

Ending Discuss with a partner any story that you found sad or shocking.

Accepting & Offering Support

Offering Help (ii)

 ☑ Children   ☑ Teenagers

Aims To build awareness of feelings about losses which have happened in peoples' lives.

Materials Large white board and coloured markers.

Warm Up Suggest that everyone works in pairs, and shares a loss they have experienced: this could relate to a pet or a person or a special possession. Remember that losing a person does not have to mean bereavement, it could be separating parents, or a friend moving away.

Focus Move to a discussion with partners about whether other people understood how you felt about this loss.

Discussion Ask the group to suggest different losses that are significant for people and write them on the white board.

Activities Now ask everyone to choose a different partner to work with, and suggest that:

✖ One person shares a loss and the other person just listens.

✖ Encourage the listeners to be 'active listeners', to be focussed and nod to show they are listening.

✖ Change roles and the sharer becomes the listener.

Sharing Did it make a difference to talk to someone who was focussed and really listened? Share your thoughts with your partner.

Ending In the whole group, talk about how we can be helpful to people who have suffered losses and whether we find it a hard thing to do.

Accepting & Offering Support

69 Do You Need Me to Listen? (i)

 Children Teenagers

> **Aims** To encourage observation of non-verbal cues in other people, and to accept constructive criticism and feedback.

> **Materials** Large white board and coloured markers.

Warm Up Invite everyone to walk round the room as if they do not want to communicate with anyone; from time to time tap on the shoulder of someone else, who should just shrug the approach off.

Focus In small groups create a body sculpt that represents 'rejection' and then create one that represents 'welcome'; move from one sculpt to the other and back again and see how the change feels.

Discussion Invite the group to suggest different gestures and expressions that keep people at a distance or discourage communication. Write all the suggestions on the board and encourage everyone to experiment physically with the different movements.

Activities Suggest that people work in threes, two role-players and one observer; role-play scenes that start in the following ways:

⊗ One person folds their arms across their chest and the other person keeps their arms by their sides.

⊗ Both people are pointing at each other in accusing ways.

⊗ One person has their arms open as if to say 'Who, me?' and the other points a warning finger.

⊗ Both people have their hands on their hips.

> **Sharing** Encourage the observer to feedback to the role-players what they noticed about the interactions. You could write statements on the white board to serve as prompts, such as: 'Who do you think was in control of the situation?', 'Was anyone sympathetic to the other person?'; 'Who needed to talk to someone with a listening ear?', 'Did the role-play feel genuine?'; and so on.

> **Ending** Suggest that people come out of role and then feedback in the whole group anything they have learned in the role-plays.

Accepting & Offering Support

Do You Need Me to Listen? (ii)

 Children  Teenagers

> **Aims** To build an awareness of the skills needed when listening to others.

> **Materials** Large white board and coloured markers.

Warm Up   Invite everyone to choose a partner, one person says 'I need to talk to you', the other responds, 'Go away, I'm busy' and walks away; repeat twice and then change over.

Focus   Still in pairs, one person now says 'I need to talk to you' and their partner responds 'OK, I'm ready to listen'; repeat, and then change over.

Discussion   In the whole group discuss, in general terms, who people feel comfortable talking to about themselves. What are the main topics that concern children or young people? Write all the responses on the white board. Remind the group that in this type of exercise, if anyone shares something personal then it must be kept confidential.

Activities   Suggest that everyone chooses a new partner and role-plays the following:

  ⊗ One person wants to talk about something, but the other is watching television.

  ⊗ One person wants to talk and the other person says, 'Yes, I want to talk to you, too'.

  ⊗ One person wants to talk and the other person answers, 'Great, what shall we talk about?'.

  ⊗ Swap roles so everyone has a turn at each character.

> **Sharing** Encourage partners to discuss which of the role-plays was most helpful to them in understanding communication from other people.

> **Ending** Suggest to the whole group that everyone closes their eyes and lets go of any feelings that may have been churned up in the roles plays, and to feel they have let go of the roles and are themselves again.

Accepting & Offering Support

71 Can I Get Through?

☑ Children ☑ Teenagers

Aims To build up the strength to find a way forward.

Materials Large white board and coloured markers, enough card and markers for everyone.

Warm Up Invite half the group to form a maze which the other half has to discover a way through – change over. Now make the maze more complex and try to negotiate the way through.

Focus Invite everyone to choose a partner and create a body-sculpt to illustrate the topic 'The Barrier'.

Discussion Using the white board, encourage everyone to contribute ideas of things that might stop them moving on, in pictures or in words.

Activities Suggest that everyone works individually with a piece of card and coloured markers to:

✪ Draw a maze that has many twists and turns but does have a way through.

✪ Change pictures with a partner and find the way through their maze, without drawing on the picture.

✪ Repeat with another partner.

✪ Draw the way through your own maze in a very strong colour.

Sharing In the whole group, take turns to show everyone your maze and discuss which were the most complex.

Ending Starting in the circle, hold hands and twist and turn around other people to make a large knot and then slowly untie it.

STOP! You Can't Go Through! (i)

☑ Children ☑ Teenagers

> **Aims** To build awareness of what stops people moving forward.

> **Materials** White board and coloured markers; strong card and markers.

Warm Up Invite everyone to walk briskly round the room, call out obstacles such as 'mud-swamp', 'electric fence', 'bramble hedge', 'rushing river' which everyone has to find a way through or over.

Focus Find partners and work together to show someone very tall standing with their arms folded and someone small and needing to pass.

Discussion Encourage a discussion of things people feel they are stopped from doing and write the ideas on the board.

Activities Suggest that everyone chooses one of the obstacles described in the warm-up:

- ⊗ Create a detailed picture of the obstacle using card and coloured markers.

- ⊗ Work with a partner and role-play a scene where one person helps the other through the obstacle, change over.

- ⊗ Repeat the exercise and find an extraordinary, 'magical' solution to overcome the obstacle.

> **Sharing** Encourage everyone to share their magical solutions in the whole group.

> **Ending** Suggest that everyone sits with their own picture of the obstacle and thinks about possible solutions.

Accepting & Offering Support

73 STOP! You Can't Go Through (ii)

 Children  Teenagers

Aims To build awareness of our personal barriers.

Materials Large white board and coloured markers, paper or card and coloured pens.

Warm Up Ask the group to divide in half, and tell one half the password for getting through an imaginary door; for example, 'green'; then tell the whole group that the password is a colour. Working in pairs, those who don't know the password must ask questions and guess what it is. Change over with a new password (e.g., wild animal, flower, month).

Focus Encourage everyone to think of as many 'knock, knock' jokes as they can and share them with a partner.

Discussion Encourage a group discussion about the doors that are closed to us, e.g., doors to after-school activities, doors to friendships. Write all the contributions on the board.

Activities Invite everyone to draw and colour their own particular locked door, the barrier that seems most insurmountable, the obstacle that makes them feel most angry or rejected; draw as much detail as possible.

Sharing Invite everyone to form twos or threes and show their pictures and talk about them; share any possible solutions.

Ending Invite everyone to share their favourite 'knock knock' joke in their twos or threes. Have you heard any good new jokes today?

Accepting & Offering Support

Helping to Find Solutions (i)

 Children  Teenagers

> **Aims** To encourage people to explore imaginative solutions to barriers.

> **Materials** Large white board and coloured markers, strong card and markers.

Warm Up Invite everyone to choose a partner and play with the idea of one person knocking on the door and the other saying, 'You can't come in because...' (e.g., you don't live here or nobody knows you) and then setting a task, such as 'You can come in if you jump up and down three times and sing a song'. It is important to keep this activity light-hearted.

Focus With a partner create 'the impossible barrier' e.g., standing face to face and pushing against each other.

Discussion Encourage everyone to contribute to the idea that 'there must be a solution' to the locked door or the barrier that is barring their way and write ideas on the board. Since the aim is about imaginative solutions, anything is acceptable.

Activities Suggest that everyone works with a partner, with sheets of card and markers:

- ⊗ Discuss and write down the 'door' you wish you could open.

- ⊗ Write down the possible reasons that it does not open.

- ⊗ Create a role-play that tests the reason; for example, 'If I did not shout and kick at the door, might someone be willing to open it?'

> **Sharing** Show in the whole group the various solutions that the pairs have explored and discuss those that could make a difference.

> **Ending** Invite everyone to create a group sculpt that shows 'perfect balance'.

Accepting & Offering Support

75 Helping to Find Solutions (ii)

☑ Children ☑ Teenagers

Aims Understanding how to set realistic goals for solutions.

Materials Large white board and coloured markers.

Warm Up Invite everyone to touch the four corners of the room, skip to the middle of the room and sing a song, and then touch six pairs of knees, in one minute! Then ask everyone to retrace their steps, reversing the actions and doing the exercise from end to beginning.

Focus Sit with a partner and talk about one small step each person would like to make in their lives. For example, someone might want to be less tired at school, so the first step could be to record a TV programme to watch later instead of staying up late.

Discussion Encourage everyone to think about how moving forward often seems so difficult that we do not even begin. Write suggestions and ideas for small steps for change on the board.

Activities Continue working with the white board and choose one task for the whole group to think about, selected from their own ideas.

For example, 'I want to join the club that I was excluded from'; discuss the reasons for an exclusion in general terms and then break down the tasks into very small steps in order to make possible the journey back. For example, if the reason for exclusion is the person was always losing their temper and hitting out, do they still lose their temper as often? Have they learnt some control? How can this be tested? Have the reasons for the temper been explored during any of these group sessions?

Sharing Talk with a partner about the next step that each person would like to make, and whether they could help each other take that step.

Ending Encourage everybody to do big physical stretches and then sit back-to-back with a partner and relax.

Helping to Find Solutions (iii)

 ✓ Children ✓ Teenagers

> **Aims** To encourage clarity of thinking about personal difficulties.

> **Materials** Large white board and coloured markers.

Warm Up Invite everyone to play a game of 'chain tag' until everyone in the group has been caught.

Focus Share with a partner one difficulty you would like to deal with now.

Discussion Remind the group that they have developed more trust and better skills for being able to listen to each other, and for collaborating together in games and tasks. Ask everyone to contribute suggestions of situations to which they would like to find solutions, and write the ideas on the board. Now invite the group to choose one situation to work on together.

Activities Suggest to the group that they form small groups of three or four people and that each group thinks of a solution to the situation, then working together:

 ✪ They can draw a before and after picture;

 ✪ Create body-sculpts to illustrate the solution;

 ✪ Create a role-play to show the solution.

> **Sharing** Encourage each group to show their solutions to the whole group, and to make constructive observations and give feedback on the ideas.

> **Ending** Suggest that in their small groups people talk about what they found helpful in the exercises.

Accepting & Offering Support

77 Who Can I Tell? (i)

☑ Children ○ Teenagers

Aims To encourage appropriate sharing of confidences.

Materials Large white board and coloured markers, sheets of card, fleecy blankets.

Warm Up In small groups, encourage everyone to play a game of hopscotch or freeze-tag.

Focus Share with a partner something that you have heard or seen on television that you thought was 'shocking' or 'too personal'.

Discussion Who do we share confidences with? Encourage a discussion of how people can feel betrayed when their best friends tell someone else a secret or some personal information. Who can we talk to if we are worried? Write ideas on the board.

Activities Invite people to form pairs, agree confidentiality, and share any situation where there has been a loss of trust between friends; then together write down one of the following:

⊗ Something I do not understand (and would like answers about).

⊗ Something I need help with (who do I ask?).

⊗ Something I need to tell someone (how do I know who to tell?).

Sharing In the whole group, encourage everyone to think about where to find answers for questions to do with school, social life or personal life.

Ending Suggest that everyone sits back-to-back with their partner, with their blankets and relaxes, breathing deeply.

Who Can I Tell? (ii)

◯ Children ☑ Teenagers

> **Aims** To encourage appropriate sharing of confidences.

> **Materials** Large white board and coloured markers.

Warm Up Walk round the group greeting everyone and taking time to 'see' everyone who is present, and remembering if anyone has had any difficulties in the past.

Focus With a partner, share a situation from the past that you wish you had told someone about.

Discussion Encourage a discussion of how people often keep things to themselves because they are scared that people will think less of them (loss of face), or they don't trust someone else to keep their confidence, or maybe someone else might get into trouble. Write examples on the board.

Activities Invite everyone to image a diagonal line across the room, with one end labelled 'I trust people' and the other 'I don't trust anyone':

✪ Ask everyone to place themselves on the line where they think they are now.

✪ Now move to where they would like to be.

✪ Observe whether anyone is surprised at where someone has placed themselves.

> **Sharing** Discuss with a partner whether you feel you can be trusted by others.

> **Ending** Sit with a partner and trust each other to give a shoulder massage.

Accepting & Offering Support

79 Do I Trust Myself?

 Children ☑ Teenagers

> **Aims** To encourage people to be aware of the limits of their own capacity to be trusted.

> **Materials** White board and coloured markers.

Warm Up Encourage everyone to choose a partner, with the expectation that they can trust their partner to take care of them. Now one person closes their eyes and the other leads them around the room as if they are a blind person, helping them to negotiate the space, shaking hands with strangers and enabling them to feel safe; change over and repeat.

Focus Share with your partner whether you felt safe with your eyes closed and also whether you felt safe doing the leading.

Discussion In the whole group, encourage a discussion about how we learn to trust other people? How much do we learn from our parents, and at what age, about being there for someone or telling the truth? (Choose appropriate information to feed into this discussion; give examples such as how you might feel if someone broke a promise or if they pretended to have something that they did not really have.)

Activities Encourage everyone to think about themselves and whether they would like people to be able to trust them:

- Create a continuum across the room, one end is 'I don't feel I can be trusted' and the other end is 'I feel you can trust me', and invite people to walk up and down the line before they choose where to place themselves.

- Think about whether you are saying that other people can't trust you or whether you are saying that you can't trust yourself.

- Now move to where you would like to be on the line and think about which of the statements you have moved away from and so which statement you have moved closer to.

> **Sharing** Talk with a partner about any uncomfortable feelings during the trust exercises, and discuss ways in which to set personal boundaries.

> **Ending** Sit back-to-back with partner, practice deep breathing and letting go of any feelings of tension.

Where Have We Got to on the Journey?

✓ Children ✓ Teenagers

Aims To encourage everyone to look at their own journey in the group, and be aware of positive changes.

Materials Large white board and coloured markers, sheets of card.

Warm Up Ask everyone to think of their favourite game or warm-up activity they have played in the group and to take turns to lead the group in that game.

Focus Form pairs and encourage everyone to discuss with their partner their favourite session and why that was.

Discussion In the whole group, encourage everyone to look back to the beginning of the group and the journey they have had up until now; write on the board favourite activities and activities people feel were important.

Activities Continue working on the board and encourage everyone to reflect on their journey, and think about what has helped them to:

✪ Think more about themselves.

✪ Think more about other people.

✪ Think more about at least some other people.

Sharing Suggest that each person tells the whole group one significant thing that has happened to them during the group sessions.

Ending Encourage everyone to make suggestions for areas that still need to be developed and write them down.

Accepting & Offering Support

Part Five
Empathy & Awareness and Moving On

Themes

81 The World's a Big Place (i)

 Children   Teenagers

Aims   To understand that moving forward need not be overwhelming.

Materials   Clay for everyone, spatulas, boards and plastic cloth, wet wipes, Worksheet 6.

Warm Up   Let everyone have a piece of clay and slap it and shape it in many different ways – nobody has to make anything specific, just play with the clay.

Focus   Make the clay as flat as possible and then as round as possible.

Discussion   Discuss with the group that everyone has their own 'world' but that actually this is made up of several worlds: our personal world, our social world, and then various others such as school or work and so on; encourage everyone to think about one of their worlds. (See also Worksheet 6.)

Activities   Now invite everyone to use their clay to create the world that they have chosen:

  ✪ Choose either your personal or your social world, and model it how you wish.

  ✪ Include positive as well as negative aspects.

  ✪ Indicate unknown areas.

  ✪ Allow the model to dry and keep until the next session.

Sharing   Discuss with a partner how it felt to work with the clay, as everyone cleans their hands with the wipes.

Ending   Discuss in the whole group the concept of seeing your world from a different perspective.

Empathy & Awareness and Moving On

The World's a Big Place (ii)

☑ Children ☑ Teenagers

Aims To develop in more detail ideas about people's individual worlds.

Materials Strong acrylic paints and brushes, water pots, extra clay for repairs, plastic mats, wet wipes, clay models from previous session, Worksheet 6.

Warm Up With children, sing and move to 'He's got the whole world in his hands'. With teenagers, invite them to choose a song about the world that they can sing and move to.

Focus Suggest that everyone sits with a partner and discuss the colours that are important for their world.

Discussion Using the models from the previous session, encourage everyone to develop a discussion about the working with clay and the concept of 'their world'. (See also Worksheet 6.)

Activities Invite everyone to decide on the colours they wish to use for their world:

⊗ Use the acrylic paints to paint the clay world.

⊗ Make sure the paints are as dry as possible to preserve the clay.

⊗ Add any patterns and shapes if needed.

⊗ Make any repairs if needed with some fresh clay.

Sharing With a partner, discuss your world and what is important in it.

Ending Discuss in the whole group how people feel about their finished worlds.

Empathy & Awareness and Moving On

This is How it Looks (i)

 Children ✓ Teenagers

Aims   To encourage participants to create their futures in an imaginative way.

Materials   Mod-roc (Plaster of Paris bandage), wooden model bases, scissors, plastic mats, wet wipes.

Warm Up   Invite everyone to sit with a partner and cut up the Mod-roc into small pieces approximately 3" x 5" (8cm x 13cm) while they share ideas about how their future will look in relation to shapes or colours in order to build a model of 'This is how it looks'.

Focus   Decide with partners whether each person will create a building or a landscape to represent 'This is how it looks'.

Discussion   Discuss with the whole group how there are some limitations when working with clay, and with these modelling materials they can create a more complex construction that can include things that will be visible and others that are hidden: in the model they may want some aspects of their future to be hidden and other aspects to be seen clearly. The Mod-roc can allow greater flexibility. Encourage questions if the instructions are not clear.

Activities   Give everyone a pile of cut Mod-roc, a water pot and model base (have some extra Mod-roc available if necessary):

✪ Create a 3D model called 'This is how it looks'.

✪ Take care not to use too much water with the Mod-roc.

✪ Smooth the surface so that it 'sticks'; create as many textures as you wish.

✪ Check that any joins are firm.

Sharing   Suggest that everyone works with a partner and discusses their model, looking at it from different sides and above; partners can ask questions to elaborate their explanations.

Ending   Suggest that people make use of the time spent clearing up of the Mod-roc to talk about their experiences; remembering to keep any spare pieces dry!

This is How it Looks (ii) 84

☑ Children ☑ Teenagers

> **Aims** To develop creative ways of looking at our lives.

> **Materials** Acrylic paints, white PVA glue, palettes, water pots and brushes, plastic mats, spare Mod-roc, scissors. Mod-roc models from the previous session.

Warm Up Place all the models from the last session in the centre of the room and encourage everyone to look at them from different angles and perspectives.

Focus With a partner, think about and discuss any changes you would like to make to your model; what is it like seeing it again? Acknowledge any feelings of disappointment or elation.

Discussion Encourage everyone to use this time to comment on their models and anything they have learned from making them. It could be that for some people this is the first time that they have managed to finish something. Compare this with their feelings about making the clay model. Check whether people want to do more to their models.

Activities Encourage each person to decide whether they want to just seal their model or to seal and paint it. Everyone can seal their models with white PVA glue, if spread thinly it will dry quickly.

- ⊗ Choose colours to paint the model, working carefully on top of the glue.

- ⊗ Make sure that the inside as well as the outside is coloured.

- ⊗ Strengthen any parts that have become fragile and need more Mod-roc.

- ⊗ Look at the model from all sides and from above.

> **Sharing** Suggest that everyone works with the partner they had earlier and share any changes and differences they can now see; encourage comments and feedback.

> **Ending** Place all the models in the centre of the room and encourage everyone to comment on differences that they can see compared with earlier observations.

85 What I Would like to Achieve (i)

 ✓ Children   ✓ Teenagers

Aims To encourage individuals to set realistic goals and implement them.

Materials Large drum, large white board and coloured markers, strong white card, Worksheet 7.

Warm Up Ask everyone to imagine they are picking cherries from a tree and that they are all very high up, so they really have to reach. Use a drum beat to create a rhythm for picking the cherries.

Focus When the drum beats a signal, create a freeze frame of how everyone is feeling right now; on another drum beat freeze how everyone would like to feel; be aware of the transition between the two.

Discussion Encourage everyone to reflect and comment on anything they feel they have achieved by being in the group; discuss the times that it felt difficult and a struggle, and when it felt hopeless and that things would not change.

Activities Show on the board (or use Worksheet 7) how to set goals and time frames for personal achievements, for example:

⊗ Create a heading: Personal Achievement.

⊗ Task: 'Greeting family members in the morning'.

⊗ Time Frame: Every day for one week.

⊗ Result: How I felt at the end of the week.

⊗ Feedback received from other people who witnessed what I was doing.

Sharing In the whole group, discuss any fears people might have that their tasks may be too difficult, and who could be around to be supportive.

Ending Talk with a partner about whether group members can be supportive of each other.

What I Would like to Achieve (ii)

 ☑ Children ☑ Teenagers

> **Aims** To encourage participants to set short-term goals and increase awareness of possibilities.

> **Materials** Large drum, large white board and coloured markers, strong card, Worksheet 8.

Warm Up Suggest that everyone walks briskly round the room and when the drum sounds once, look downwards, on the next drum beat look backwards, then look forwards. With a partner imagine one person is holding something that is 'just out of reach' and the other person must try to chase it or stretch up for it, but it is just beyond them.

Focus Working with a partner, discuss specific school-based goals and achievements that could be aimed at during the next week.

Discussion In the whole group encourage the pairs to reveal their ideas for goals and achievements that could be set for the immediate future, write all the ideas on the board and feedback. Discuss when an idea is perhaps unrealistic in the short term.

Activities On the board draw a simple table or diagram (or use Worksheet 8) to show a goal and a time frame. For example, In School:

⊗ Heading: 'Achievement' (or Goal).

⊗ 'Paying quiet attention in class'.

⊗ Time frame: One whole day.

⊗ Result: Did I achieve what I set out to?

⊗ Feedback: Any comments from teacher(s).

> **Sharing** Discuss with a partner whether they can give each other mutual support to achieve success.

> **Ending** Invite members of the group to choose a closing exercise.

87 What I Would like to Achieve (iii)

 Children Teenagers

Aims To encourage group members to give each other feedback.

Materials Large white board and coloured markers, strong white card, Worksheets 7 and 8.

Warm Up Everyone sits in a circle and at a signal stands up one at a time; if two people stand up together then the game must start over again, until the group works together to achieve their goal.

Focus Invite the group to stand in a circle and to look carefully around at everyone as if for the first time; pair off in twos and give each other a positive comment about anything they have observed.

Discussion Encourage everyone to contribute to a discussion about what others have achieved in the group. (See also Worksheets 7 and 8.)

Activities Suggest that everyone continues with the same partner and works to develop the confidence to feedback about each other's behaviour:

- ✪ One person listens while their partner describes something that person does that they find really irritating, then the listener says how they feel.

- ✪ Change round and repeat the exercise.

- ✪ One person listens and their partner describes something they really appreciate about them, then the listener says how they feel.

- ✪ Change round and repeat the exercise.

Sharing With a new partner, share the observations and what can be learned from this exercise.

Ending Sit back-to-back with a partner, feel the support as you breathe slowly and deeply.

A Map to Take with Me (i)

 Children  Teenagers

Aims	To encourage everyone to be aware of what moves them forward and what pulls them back.

Materials	Large drum, large white board and coloured markers, strong white card.

Warm Up   Invite everyone to spread out and move across the room, when the drum beats they will encounter different things in the landscape such as: 'a straight easy road', 'a dark forest', 'a swamp that sucks you in', 'a winding path'.

Focus   With a partner, think about difficulties that might be encountered on a journey, for example, not being able to see the way ahead, going it alone.

Discussion   Encourage everyone to give examples of times when 'the going gets tough', such as: being teased for not drinking or when an adult has not kept a promise. Write the examples on the board and suggest that these could become the difficult areas of a map.

Activities   Invite everyone to create their own personal map of their life journey. With the card and markers, create a map of the road or path for the future.

- ❊ Draw and colour areas that represent difficulties and struggles, such as swamps, deep rivers, pits, barriers.

- ❊ Draw and colour areas that are easier, where the path seems clear, where there might be other people who could help, maybe somewhere to pause and take time.

Sharing	Suggest everyone sits with a partner and shares their map and discusses the difficult areas.

Ending	In the whole group, discuss whether for some people their maps feel too difficult, and perhaps they need some assistance to include more ideas for resources.

Empathy & Awareness and Moving On

89 A Map to Take with Me (ii)

○ Children ✓ Teenagers

Aims To acknowledge that the future could present difficulties.

Materials Large drum, large white board and coloured markers, large sheets of card, PVA glue, scissors, assorted newspapers and magazines.

Warm Up Encourage members of the group to lead a warm up with a variation on a previous exercise, using the drum if they wish.

Focus Create a body sculpt with the whole group where everyone is free and then where everyone represents a hurdle or barrier; change from one to the other.

Discussion In the whole group discuss how change can be difficult and scary and often people will stay in a situation that is unsatisfactory, rather than face an unknown future. Write suggestions and examples on the board.

Activities Suggest that everyone works in small groups of three people and together create a collage of the 'map of the future' idea: give each group a sheet of card, newspapers and magazines, glue and scissors, coloured markers:

⊗ Cut out from newspapers headings or phrases or messages, both positive and negative.

⊗ Find appropriate pictures, for example, doors or barriers, storms and so on.

⊗ Put them together to form the map and stick on the card, colour any spaces, add symbols such as hearts to represent support or signposts to suggest danger.

Sharing Show the maps to the whole group and compare similarities and differences. Encourage people to make suggestions if some of the difficulties need more balance.

Ending If people would like, the maps can be photocopied so that everyone has one to keep. In the groups of three, sit back-to-back and feel supported by the other people and breathe deeply.

Empathy & Awareness and Moving On

My Map for the Journey

 Children Teenagers

Aims	To address issues of anxiety about change.

Materials	Large white board and coloured markers, large sheet of strong paper, scissors and glue.

Warm Up   Encourage the group to lead the warm up, either based on a previous exercise or introducing a game of their own.

Focus   In pairs, discuss ideas about how people can support each other when the future becomes scary.

Discussion   Introduce ideas (or show pictures) of ancient maps that had pictures of the winds blowing, unknown lands, labels reading 'Here be dragons', strange fish in the sea, ships breaking up on rocks, and discuss these. Write these ideas on the board and discuss how they might relate to people's thoughts for the future.

Activities   Invite the group to create one large map on a strong piece of paper, and divide into small groups to work on different sections such as:

- ✪ An outline of the whole map.

- ✪ Colouring in the sea or land.

- ✪ Creating the rocks and a wrecked ship.

- ✪ Creating the unknown lands and naming them.

- ✪ Showing where the fish or the winds and so on are placed.

Sharing	Invite everyone to share in the whole group their achievement and how it felt to work together in both the small and large groups.

Ending	Discuss in the group their connections with the map and their feelings about the future.

Empathy & Awareness and Moving On

91 Is There Anybody There? (i)

 Children ☑ Teenagers

> **Aims** Dealing with situations when doors to opportunities remain closed.

> **Materials** Large white board and coloured markers, copies of the poem 'The Listeners' by Walter de la Mare.

Warm Up Invite members of the group to lead a new warm-up that they have brought to the groups from outside (encourage people to work in pairs).

Focus What happens and how do people feel when a door to an opportunity stays closed? Discuss with a partner different situations when this could happen.

Discussion Encourage discussion in the whole group about how it feels when doors we would like to open stay closed? Are they doors to the future? A door to someone that might help us? A door to a friend? Write suggestions on the board.

Activities Invite everyone to sit comfortably in a circle or back-to-back with a partner, and read the first half of the poem by Walter de la Mare, 'The Listeners' down to the line: '*By the lonely Traveller's call*' and repeat it, encouraging everyone to follow the text on their copy.

⊗ Invite a discussion about who this 'lonely Traveller' might be, and who he thinks is living in the big house? How much can we know about the situation from the poem? Which words give us the clues?

> **Sharing** Continue to discuss in the whole group whether or not people like poetry, and whether they might grow to like certain types of poem and perhaps try to write poems of their own.

> **Ending** Sit back-to-back with a partner while the whole poem is read to the end.

Is There Anybody There? (ii)

☑ Children ☑ Teenagers

Aims To be able to express feelings about times when there is 'no-one there'.

Materials Large white board and coloured markers, strong white card, copies of 'Don't Talk to Me – a Teenage Rap' (see Worksheet 9), copies of a dictionary of rhymes.

Warm Up Continue to encourage the group to lead their own warm-ups.

Focus Share with a partner how difficult it can sometimes be to find the right words to express feelings.

Discussion Encourage group members to contribute as many words and phrases as they can to express how they feel when life is difficult. The teenage rap on Worksheet 9, 'Don't Talk to Me', is a good example: it starts 'Don't touch me / Don't talk to me / I don't want your empathy'.

Activities Suggest that everyone looks at the words and phrases on the board and writes down any that connect with their own feelings and life events, and feelings of being alone:

⊗ Think of as many words as possible that rhyme with them (use the dictionary if needed).

⊗ Put together the words and phrases to make your own rap or poem about feeling alone.

⊗ Write this out neatly on a sheet of card.

⊗ Decorate and sign your poem or rap.

Sharing Continue with the same partner and share the words that you found to use: read out loud each other's poem.

Ending Discuss in the whole group how it felt to create a poem or rap of your own, did it really express your feelings?

Empathy & Awareness and Moving On

93 Feelings that Get in the Way

 Children   Teenagers

> **Aims** To continue giving form to feelings through poems and raps.

> **Materials** Large white board and coloured markers, large white card, newspapers and magazines, scissors and PVA glue.

Warm Up Continue to encourage group members to lead the warm up and now to accept feedback from other group members on their communication skills.

Focus Encourage everyone to explore with a partner how they deal with feelings such as jealousy or resentment. Who do they have these feelings towards and why?

Discussion Invite everyone to share any feelings they have of jealousy or resentment of other people and their possessions; do we put people down because they have something we do not? Write the responses on the board.

Activities Continue the theme of rapping or writing and invite everyone in the group to use words and pictures from magazines and newspapers to create their own rap or poem:

- ✪ Look for headlines and pictures on the theme of 'jealousy' or 'resentment'.

- ✪ Cut out short phrases, exclamations and pictures.

- ✪ Stick these on a piece of card to create your own individual expression in the form of a rap or poem.

- ✪ Decorate with coloured markers and sign it with your personal signature.

> **Sharing** In pairs show and read your poem to your partner and give constructive feedback.

> **Ending** Relax back-to-back and feel a sense of achievement about what you have created.

The Most Difficult Things Is... (i)

◯ Children   ☑ Teenagers

> **Aims**   To continue to give form to feelings through role-play.

> **Materials**   Large white board and coloured markers, hats, caps, scarves and cloths.

Warm Up   Encourage group members to lead warm ups that focus on words and facial expressions.

Focus   Invite everyone to work with a partner and explore the topic of 'pressure' in their lives.

Discussion   Encourage everyone to talk about the pressures they feel, both general and specific, that come from adults: to change behaviour, ways of dressing, ways of talking, not to smoke, not to drink, to come home early. Write all the ideas on the board and underline those that people feel are the most common pressures.

Activities   Suggest that everyone works in small groups of three and together create a role-play scene or sculpt (using hats and other props if needed) that shows one of the following:

- ✪ The pressure to change.

- ✪ The pressure to succeed.

- ✪ The pressure to compete.

- ✪ Show it to the whole group and invite comments. Invite other group members to suggest an appropriate change by moving something in the sculpt or bringing a new character into the role-play.

> **Sharing**   In the whole group discuss whether the changes made a difference, and whether there is one small change we could make in our lives to reduce our own pressures.

> **Ending**   Introduce a relaxation exercise where everyone sits on the floor back-to-back with someone, and as they breathe deeply, imagine that each of the pressures in their lives is slipping away.

95 The Most Difficult Thing is... (ii)

 Children Teenagers

Aims To acknowledge real difficulties of peer pressure.

Materials Large white board and coloured markers.

Warm Up Suggest to group members that they work together create a warm-up that shows physically the pressures and burdens on their shoulders.

Focus In pairs, one person presses down on the shoulders of the other so they really feel the weight; change over.

Discussion Explore in the whole group how difficult it is to explain to your friends the pressures they can put you under; encourage everyone to contribute ideas about the expectations of friends to do the things that they do. Explain the concept of 'peer pressure'.

Activities Suggest that everyone divides into small groups of three or four to discuss 'peer pressure'.

- ✪ Discuss the positive aspects of belonging to a peer group.

- ✪ Share the negative aspects of belonging to a peer group.

- ✪ Explore what it must feel like not to belong to a peer group.

- ✪ Choose one situation to create in a role-play.

Sharing Invite the small groups to work with another group to explore together the ideas of peer pressure.

Ending Check whether anyone in the small groups has been affected by the discussions or role-plays and find ways to reassure them in the whole group and through support from the group.

You Remind Me of... (i)   96

☑ Children   ☑ Teenagers

> **Aims** To give form to feelings about other people.

> **Materials** Large white board and coloured markers, large sheets of white card, newspapers and magazines, scissors and PVA glue.

Warm Up Suggest that everyone stands in a circle and takes it in turns to say to the person on their right a demanding statement such as: 'I am your teacher, where is your homework', 'I am your mother, why haven't you done the washing up?' – the person does not reply, but instead turns and asks their own question.

When you have been all the way round the circle, go around again but this time phrase the same statement in a less demanding way, e.g., 'I am your teacher, please remember your homework', 'I am your mother, I do need your help with the washing up'.

Focus Suggest that people talk in pairs about someone who concerns them, either a family member or a friend. They maybe concerned about the person's health or because they seem preoccupied, or because they seem to have changed in some way.

Discussion Continue the discussion in the whole group and think about the difficulties of caring for some else when that person also makes demands; write on the board the people we worry about most and whether we are able to show our feelings towards them.

Activities Encourage group members to create a college from newspaper and magazine pictures:

- ✪ Cut out pictures that remind people of friends and relatives, both those who group members feel close to and those from whom they feel distanced or estranged.

- ✪ Before sticking the pictures on the collage, play with different groupings such as: grouping family members together, and friends further away, change them round.

- ✪ If anyone has two families, include both of them.

> **Sharing** With a partner, show each other your collage and talk about which person in the picture you feel closest to, and which you feel most distant from.

> **Ending** In the whole group, share examples of people who group members would perhaps like to get to know and ideas of how to begin the process.

97 You Remind Me Of... (ii)

 ☑ Children ☑ Teenagers

Aims To continue giving form to feelings about people we care about.

Materials Large white board and coloured markers.

Warm Up Continue to encourage group members to lead the warm-ups and to accept feedback from others on their communication skills.

Focus In pairs discuss how difficult it is to care for someone else.

Discussion Encourage everyone in the group to contribute ideas about caring for other people: perhaps group members have a sibling or parent with disabilities or mental ill-health. Discuss how difficult it is to tell other people about relatives who have special needs. Write all the ideas on the board.

Activities Invite everyone in the group to imagine how it feels to have someone in the family who needs help:

✪ Granny who is becoming forgetful.

✪ Parent who is depressed.

✪ Sibling who has disabilities.

✪ Choose one situation to role-play in small groups, and explore how people feel.

Sharing Discuss in small groups how this becomes a different sort of pressure: keeping things about home a secret, being late for school, being teased by other people.

Ending Explore in the whole group how it feels to know that some has a relative with such needs: is it possible to feel empathy for them?

If Only Things Could be Different!

 Children   Teenagers

Aims To understand how feelings of 'if only' can dictate how people act.

Materials Large white board and coloured markers, large sheets of white card, newspapers and magazines, scissors and PVA glue.

Warm Up In pairs, take it in turns to give each other different ways of moving around the room, call out changes that your partner has to follow, such as: 'walk like a baby' or 'run like an athlete' or 'crawl like a wounded animal'.

Focus With a partner, discuss how often you use the phrase 'if only' as in: 'If only I lived with my dad...' or 'If only I could change school...'

Discussion Invite everyone to contribute to a discussion about wanting things to change in other people, or in the world outside and how difficult it is to acknowledge changes that we need to make for ourselves. One of the difficulties is that we sometimes try to change everything at once! Write everyone's ideas for 'If only's' and for possible small changes on the board.

Activities Encourage the group to form small groups of three or four, and choose a small change that they could try out:

- ✪ Create a group sculpt that shows the before and after of the change.
- ✪ Develop this into a role-play to illustrate the change.
- ✪ Make sure that everyone has the opportunity to play the person who is changing.

Sharing Discuss whether this small change is possible or does it need to be made even more simple? Are there other small changes that could be made that do not feel too daunting?

Ending Resolve in the small group to use the phrase 'If only' less often!

 Ⓟ This page may be photocopied for instructional use only. *101 Activities for Empathy & Awareness* © Sue Jennings 2011

Empathy & Awareness and Moving On

99 Achievements & Celebrations (i)

 Children Teenagers

> **Aims** To give form to feelings about being appreciated and showing appreciation.

> **Materials** Large white board, card folded like a greetings card, glitter glue, coloured pens and decorations.

Warm Up Continue to encourage group members to lead the warm-ups and to accept feedback from other group members on their communication skills.

Focus How do we show our appreciation of someone else?

Discussion Encourage a discussion on the topic, 'If we have been appreciated then we can show appreciation to other people'.

Activities Invite everyone to write their name on a small piece of paper and put it in a hat or basket – shuffle these and then ask everyone to pick a name:

❂ Think about the person whose name you have, and their positive qualities.

❂ Create a greetings card for this person that gives positive feedback. Write the person's name on the back of the card.

❂ Place all the cards face down, so the person's name shows on the back.

❂ Everyone takes the card with their name on and reads through what is inside; if possible, try to keep the exercise anonymous.

❂ Relax and absorb the positive feedback.

> **Sharing** In small groups discuss how people felt when given their card.

> **Ending** Relax back-to-back and feel a sense of achievement about what has been said about you.

Empathy & Awareness and Moving On

Achievements & Celebrations (ii)

 Children ✓ Teenagers

> **Aims** To acknowledge achievement and success.

> **Materials** Large white board and coloured markers, large white card, Worksheet 10.

Warm Up Continue to encourage group members to lead the warm-ups and to accept feedback from other group members on their communication skills.

Focus Discuss with a partner all the things that have been modelled or created in the sessions, and think about what you will do with your pictures and models.

Discussion Explore situations when we say goodbye and invite group members to contribute examples of times when they have not been able to say goodbye. Write examples on the board. (See also Worksheeet 10.)

Activities Explore in small groups the difficulties that may arise from ending this group, and ways of saying goodbye to others:

    ⊗ Create a goodbye picture for the whole group.

    ⊗ Discuss people who will be missed from the group.

    ⊗ Talk about what group members will do after the group is finished.

> **Sharing** In the whole group feedback and discuss what people will find difficult about leaving the group.

> **Ending** For the final relaxation exercise allow the group to choose their favourite.

Empathy & Awareness and Moving On

101 Celebration of Achievement

 Children   Teenagers

> **Aims** To affirm everyone's progress and achievements.

> **Materials** Large white board and coloured markers, certificates of skills achieved in the workshop with each person's name on (see Worksheets 10 and 11).

Warm Up Encourage group members to lead the warm-up and suggest a theme of 'hello and goodbye'.

Focus In pairs, share the most important decision they have made about 'moving on' in their lives.

Discussion Encourage the whole group to share ideas for celebrations such as favourite games, warm-ups, role-plays and stories.

Activities Invite everyone to suggest their favourite activity from the group (you will probably get duplicates):

- ✪ Create a whizz-through of the programme with brief versions of favourite things.

- ✪ Allow space for discussing those activities that people did not enjoy.

- ✪ Build up to the climax of the presentation of Certificates of Achievement for each participant.

> **Sharing** Encourage everyone to share their thoughts as the programme ends.

> **Ending** Let the whole group give a loud and sustained clap and cheer for everyone.

Resources

Worksheets

Useful Reading

Music for Relaxation

Music for Rhythms

Can You Read Your Palm?

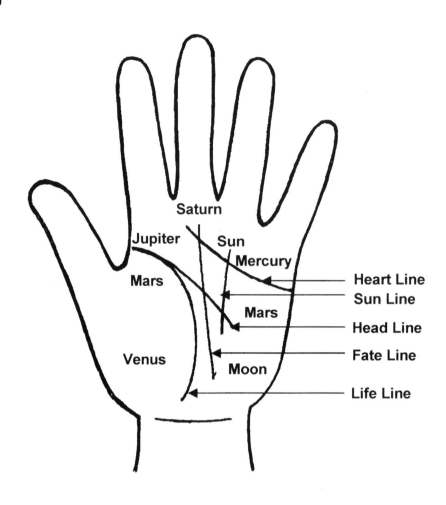

Saturn

Jupiter   Sun
              Mercury

Mars   Heart Line
                              Sun Line
              Mars
                              Head Line

Venus   Fate Line
              Moon

                              Life Line

1 Your left hand is supposed to be all about your past.

2 Look at your left hand and see how it compares with the picture.

3 Fill in the blank picture so it looks like yours.

4 Write down what you thought about while looking at your palm.

_____

_____

_____

_____

_____

Getting the Balance Right

1 Make a list of all the things in your life that seem 'difficult' (choose from school, family, friends).

2 Make a list of all the things that are OK in your life.

3 Make a list of all the things that are great in your life.

If these things were put on the scales, where would the most weight be?

Complete the sentences:

The thing that weighs most in my life is _____

_____

A way that I can change it is _____

_____

What is stopping me make this change _____

_____

WORKSHEET 2: ACTIVITY 14

Different Types of Spaces

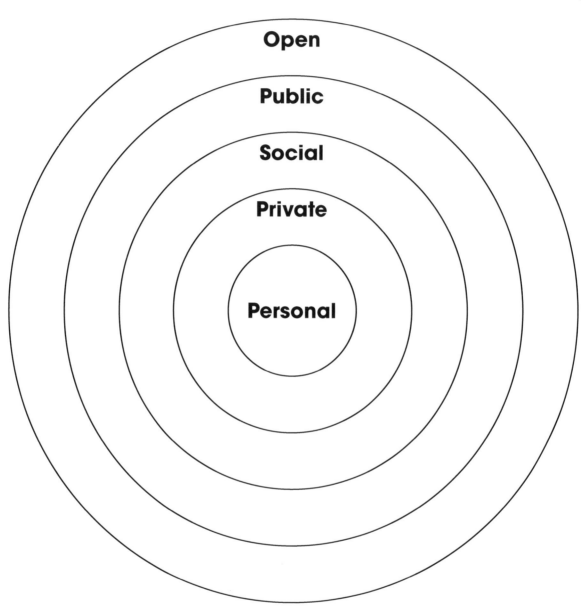

Open

Public

Social

Private

Personal

✪ Write in each of the circles where the space is and what type of activities belong in that space

✪ Write who inhabits or is allowed into these spaces.

✪ Write in anything you would like to say about the difference spaces.

The Mask of Fear

1 Think about a time that you were frightened of something.

2 What colour would the mask of fear be?

3 Create your own mask of fear by colouring the blank mask.

4 Write a short story or a few sentences about overcoming the fear.

_____

_____

_____

_____

_____

_____

The Time-Line of My Life

1 Trace over the time line in colour and add any twists or corners that you have had in your life as far back as you can remember.

2 Write your age at different points along the way.

3 Mark any important times from your life.

4 Add any important features such as woods, houses, dangerous places or straight lines.

How to Reach the Island

1 Develop the picture of the island using the following ideas:

✪ Colour the trees and add more if you want.

✪ Think about who lives on the island.

✪ Where do they live and what do they do?

2 How can you get to the island? By boat, by swimming, in a plane?

✪ Why do people want to reach the island?

✪ What will they do there?

✪ Will they stay or leave again?

Personal Achievements 1

Set yourself a task within a time frame (such as saying good morning to your family every day for a week). Write down the task and time frame below and at the end of the time write down any reaction from people who have seen what you achieved.

Task: _____

_____

Time Frame: _____

Reactions from others who have seen what I have achieved: _____

_____

_____

My own reactions to what I achieved: _____

_____

_____

Personal Achievements 2

Set yourself a task within your school setting, with a time frame, such as sitting still or not distracting others for a whole day (and then getting feedback from teachers or others around you).

Task: _____

_____

Time Frame: _____

Reactions from other people, such as teachers: _____

_____

_____

My own reactions to what I achieved: _____

_____

_____

WORKSHEET 9 ACTIVITY 92
Don't Talk to Me – A Teenage Rap

Don't touch me

Don't talk to me

I don't need your empathy

Just leave me alone

Just let me be angry

You don't know what it's like to be me

You don't know the red mist I see

You don't know the clenched fist when your head's a mess

You don't know what to do when there are no words left

My mouth can't speak

But my body roars

It's a weapon of mass destruction

It's a raging inner war

Becky, from the Actionwork Project

The Mask of Adventure

1   Think of an adventure you would like to have.

2   What colour would the 'adventure' mask be?

3   Create your own mask of adventure by colouring the blank mask.

4   Write a short story or a few sentences about the adventure you could have in the mask.

_____

_____

_____

_____

_____

_____

Certificate of Achievement

Certificate of Achievements

Awarded to

_____

has shown skills in the following areas:

_____

_____

and has contributed to the group by:

_____

_____

_____   _____
Signed   Date

Friendship Circles

1 Colour in the circles in any way you want.

2 Think about the way these circles overlap each other.

3 Imagine one circle is you, decide who the other circles could be: members of your family, friends or other people at school?

4 Write the names of important people inside the circles

WORKSHEET
13 Friendship Tree

1 Colour in the tree in any way you want.

2 Think about people who are important in your life.

3 Write the names of these important people inside the circles on the tree.

4 Do these people know how important they are in your life?

Useful Reading

Barstow, C., 2005, *Right Use of Power*, Boulder CO: Many Realms Publishing.

Collmar, L., 2010, *Seeing through the Eyes of Another: Stories for seeing life from different perspectives*, Buckingham: Hinton House Publishers.

Collmar, L., 2010, *Walking in the Shoes of Another: Stories for seeing life from different perspectives*, Buckingham: Hinton House Publishers.

Gibb, B., 2007, *The Rough Guide to the Brain: get to know your grey matter*, London: Rough Guides.

Gil, E., 1991, *The Healing Power of Play*, New York: Guilford Press.

Gordon, M., 2009, *Roots of Empathy*, New York: The Experiment Publishing Company.

Grainger, R., 2010, *Suspending Disbelief: Theatre as a Context for Sharing*, Brighton: Sussex Academic Press.

Hughes, D., 2006, *Building the Bonds of Attachment: Awakening Love in Deeply Troubled Children*, Lanham MD: Jason Aronson.

Jennings, S., 2004, *Creative Storytelling with Children at Risk*, Milton Keynes: Speechmark Publishing.

Jennings, S., 2005a, *Creative Storytelling with Adults at Risk*, Milton Keynes: Speechmark Publishing.

Jennings, S., 2005b, *Creative Play with Children at Risk*, Milton Keynes: Speechmark Publishing.

Jennings, S., 2010, *StoryBuilding: 100+ Ideas for Developing Story & Narrative Skills*, Buckingham: Hinton House Publishers.

Lupton, H., 2008, *Tales of Wisdom and Wonder*, Bath: Barefoot Books.

Pinel, J., with Edwards, M., 2008, *A Colourful Introduction to the Anatomy of the Human Brain*, London: Pearson Education.

Sunderland, M., 2008, *Smasher: A story to help adolescents with anger & alienation*, Buckingham: Hinton House Publishers.

Sunderland, M. (ed.), 2011, *Helping Teenagers with Anger and Low Self-Esteem*, Buckingham: Hinton House Publishers.

Music for Relaxation

Aeoliah, 1995, *Healing Music for Reiki 1*, Aerdenhout: Oreade Music.

Llewellyn, 2006, *Sleep Gold: Music to Aid Restful Sleep*, Tring: Paradise Music.

Lovland, R., & Sherry, F., 1992, *Songs from a Secret Garden*, Oslo: Phillips.

Oldfield, T., 1993, *Out of the Depths*, Halesworth: New World Music.

Music for Rhythms

Gordon, S., & G., 1998, *Sacred Spirit Drums*, Cardiff-By-The-Sea CA: Sequoia Records.

Kodo, 1994, *The Best of Kodo*, Athens: Tristar.

101
ONE HUNDRED AND ONE
Activities & Ideas

✱ Creative and practical solutions to issues around emotional well-being in young people. Many teachers, care workers and therapists are challenged by difficult behaviours, and families often feel lost for solutions to sudden outbursts or young people's feelings of alienation and lack of self-esteem.

✱ Containing a host of ideas for home, school and youth groups, the books will help to tackle these difficult issues in a positive and active way. There are no magic answers, but the ideas aim to empower young people to find solutions to some of their own difficulties, while providing guidance for more positive directions.

✱ The books adopt a 'hands-on' approach with a firm and enabling attitude and provide a sound practical basis for active intervention for behaviour change.

**101 Activities for
Empathy & Awareness**
ISBN: 978-1-906531-33-1

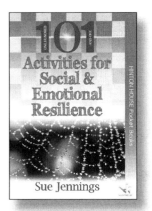

**101 Activities for Social
& Emotional Resilience**
ISBN: 978-1-906531-46-1

**101 Ideas for Managing
Challenging Behaviour**
ISBN: 978-1-906531-44-7

**101 Activities for Increasing
Focus & Motivation**
ISBN: 978-1-906531-45-4

**101 Activities for Positive
Thoughts & Feelings**
ISBN: 978-1-906531-47-8

www.hintonpublishers.com

The 50 Best Games series …

☼ These handy pocket books will ensure you are never again stuck for activity ideas that will help make both teaching and learning fun!

☼ Carefully selected, each collection of the 50 Best Games is themed and addresses a specific area of development. All the games are easy to implement with the minimum of preparation and can be adapted to the needs of your particular group.

☼ Use them as warm-ups, ice breakers, time fillers or to address a specific need. Suitable for groups of all sizes and can be used with all ages from young children to adolescents.

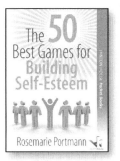

The 50 Best Games for Building Self-Esteem

ISBN 978-0-906531-18-8

The 50 Best Perception Games

ISBN 978-0-906531-11-9

The 50 Best Games for Brain Exercise

ISBN 978-0-906531-14-0

The 50 Best Games for Relaxation & Concentration

ISBN 978-0-906531-17-1

The 50 Best Games for Speech & Language Development

ISBN 978-0-906531-13-3

The 50 Best Games for Children's Groups

ISBN 978-0-906531-12-6

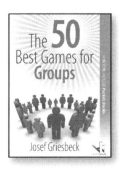

The 50 Best Games for Groups

ISBN 978-0-906531-16-4

The 50 Best Indoor Games for Groups

ISBN 978-0-906531-15-7

www.hintonpublishers.com